Phil

Sally Brush.

5.11.11.

CERRIGYDRUDION 1662–1812
An Incomplete Jigsaw

Sally Brush

© Sally Brush

ISBN: 978-1-84524-

Cover design: Eirian Evans

First edition: 2011
Llygad Gwalch, Ysgubor Plas, Llwyndyrys,

☎: 01758 750432   ▤: 01758 750438

✆: llyfrau@carreg-gwalch.com
Website: www.carreg-gwalch.com

Sally Brush was born and brought up on the edge of South London before moving to be nearer her mother's family in Lincolnshire. This is where her interest in local history began. After teaching for five years she trained for the ministry and was ordained Deaconess in the Church in Wales in 1976, beginning in Flint. In 1980 she was one of the first five women to be ordained Deacon. Between 1983-1987 she served as Minor Canon of St Asaph Cathedral, before being appointed as the first woman to be in charge of a group of churches based around Cerrigydrudion, she was with the first group of women to be ordained priest in St Asaph Cathedral in 1987. She was awarded her M. Phil. in 1996. In her spare time she researched for her Ph.D. which was awarded the year after her retirement in 2008. This book is based on the research around her Ph.D.

Doing the research for my Ph.D. and writing this book is rather like doing a jigsaw without the picture and with no knowledge to start with of how many pieces there are! Some records and information are very good, others very patchy and frustratingly, some non-existent. For example the records of baptisms, weddings and funerals are very good and clear, whereas the records for the overseer of the poor have been lost somewhere. Hunting around one finds 'little gems' that have been added in and which often throw interesting light on an individual or a situation. All in all it has been most interesting to write and I would like to thank all the people who have helped me in a variety of ways. Diolch yn fawr iawn.

Sally Brush

Contents

Introduction

Doing the research for my Ph.D and then sorting things out for this book was, in many ways similar to doing a puzzle, such as a crossword or jigsaw or reading a detective story. Any sort of research is dependant on the material available and the ability to interpret it. The Clwyd Family History Society had transcribed the old church registers and typed them up, making them accessible to the general public. The register recording baptisms, marriages and funerals for Cerrigydrudion begins in 1590 and is still kept up to the present day. The information from 1662 onwards includes enough information to make it possible to identify a very large number of people and to make family trees, some for up to four generations. These showed the date people were married, the date their children were baptised and the date of their funeral. Having made family trees it was then possible to look up documents at the Denbighshire Record Office in Ruthin and start to link people together. For example, the Thomas Parry Charity Book lists the people who were given money which gives some idea of who the poorer people were. Some were listed as widows and it was possible to check this with the burial register. However, this book is called 'An Incomplete Jigsaw' because of the gaps in information. The records of the Overseers of the Poor have disappeared and so there is little other information about the poor. The Denbighshire Session Rolls for the eighteenth century are available and these throw light on the sort of crimes committed and who the perpetrators were. There were many odd pieces of information where which all helped to build up the total picture.

There were many other documents stored at the National Library in Aberystwyth including all the church records. These reports, letters and official information give a good insight in the church's role in the community, who the clergy were and what they did and a wide variety of odds and ends that filled in gaps in the total picture. All the wills, inventories and bonds for Cerrigydrudion are stored there and provided a wealth of information about people's possessions, money and family relationships. The records of the Great Sessions, which dealt with more serious crimes, are kept there. Very few related to Cerrigydrduion, but they included an accusation of infanticide and another of forgery.

There were some interesting moments. Reading through the wills I came across one for Anne Jones. As I read it through it became clear that she had left money to her niece and nephews, one being Jac Glan Gors. I also looked at a book of Welsh sermons attributed to Dr. William Worthington, Rector of Llanrhaeadr ym Mochnant, but a careful study of this small, calf bound book and comparison with other documents written by Rev. Peter Powell, showed it had been written by him. He was a curate in Cerrigydrudion 1722-1726! (You will find more information about him in the chapter called 'Meet The 'People')

St. Mary Magdalen Church in Cerrigydrudion has a number of interesting plaques on the walls and it was possible to identify the people named and find out a bit about them. A number of people locally helped identify houses that were now in ruins and helped to work out old roads and routes. There are a good number of academic books written about the eighteenth century which tallied with the information I had found, some of which was quite surprising. For example, people did not usually get married until their mid to late twenties and only had four or five children. This changed in the nineteenth century when people began to get married at a much younger age and often had families of ten or more children. Most books written about eighteenth century Wales have concentrated on south Wales and have assumed that north Wales would be similar. This is particularly true with regard to the church which was in a desperate state of poverty and decline in the south, but the situation was much better in the north, which is certainly one of the reasons why non-conformity did not start to grow until the turn of the nineteenth century.

There were also articles in various historical magazines which helped to fill in small parts of the jigsaw. Around 1695 Edward Lhwyd, an antiquarian historian, sent a questionnaire to the clergy in north Wales asking for a variety of information including anything unusual in their parishes. David Wynne, the Rector replied and included a note saying, *'Sion Browling o Nant y Krogwr oedh 96.'* (Sion Browling of Nant y Krogwr is 96 years old). The Burial Book records his burial on 6 February 1696. He also mentions *'mae Bwyain bres gan Reinalt Jones yn ymyl eglwys Kerrig.'* (Reinalt Jones has a brass axe near the church.) A puzzling piece, as neither Reinalt Jones nor the axe, are mentioned elsewhere.

Surnames, as we know them now, were virtually unknown in north Wales during this period. Children were given a first name followed by 'ap' or vch' (son or daughter of) followed by their father's first name. So, Robert ap David's children would have been Owen ap Robert and Lowry vch Robert. As time went by the ap and vch were often dropped and the second name had an 's' added to it, making Roberts, Williams and Johnes, or Jones. In a small community this system worked well. When girls got married they kept their name, making it easy to identify people There was no standardisation of the spelling of words or of people's names. Ellen, for example, was spelt, Ellin, Elen, Elin and even Eleanor and Cadwaladr was often shortened to Cadd'r and sometimes spelt with a 'k' One person could have their name spelt, Ellen vch David, Elin Davies or even Eleanor Dafydd.

Without all the help I received from the Denbighshire Record Office, Ruthin Library and The National Library of Wales as well as many people locally this book would not have been written. I would like to thank them, as well as Elena Williams, Betws Gwerfyl Goch, who typed my Ph.D , Helen Williams who typed this book and Philip Kynaston for his computer skills.

At the end of each chapter are end notes which give further information about where things came from.

NLW. National Library Of Wales, Aberystwyth.
DRO. Denbighshire Record Office, Ruthin.

For those floundering with old money!:

12d (pence) = 1s (shilling) 2 0s = £
Quite a lot of things were valued in guineas. £1-1s-0d.

Chapter 1

CERRIGYDRUDION NOW AND THEN

The village of Cerrigydrudion is in north Wales, ten miles from Corwen, twelve from Betws y Coed, eleven from Bala and fourteen from Ruthin.

In the twenty first century it has been by-passed by the A5 and would be seen as a small collection of houses and bungalows, surrounded by beautiful countryside and scattered farms with a population of about 600. In comparison with all the neighbouring, smaller villages, it still has a grocer shop which has the Post Office. The doctor's surgery, bank, garage and library and retained fire station are all based in the village, along with a variety of small businesses. There are two cafes, but only one public house, the other having closed in the last fifteen years. It still has a Primary School and the school building is used by the community for a wide variety of meetings, clubs and events.

The three medieval churches in the area, Cerrigydrudion, Betws Gwerfyl Goch and Llanfihangel Glyn Myfyr are still open as well as churches in Ysbyty Ifan, Pentrefoelas and Maerdy. There are ten Welsh Presbyterian and four Annibynwyr chapels. One Presbyterian, and one Annibynwyr and the only Wesley Methodist chapel have all closed in the last ten years.

Because of the wide variety of services still available in the village, people come from neighbouring communities to use the shops and other facilities. It is still a dominantly Welsh speaking area with a few English incomers.

The village in 1662 had a population of around 400, of whom

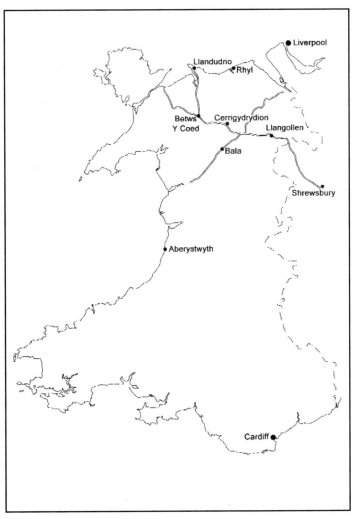

A map showing Wales and the position of Cerrigydrudion.[1]

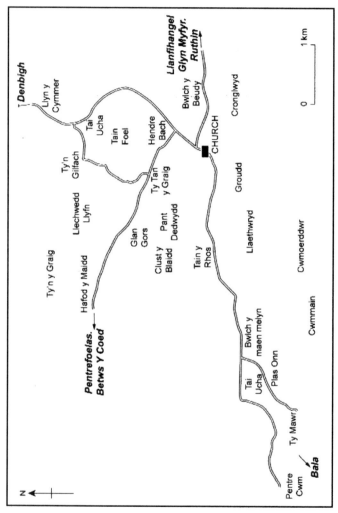

A more detailed map of the village around 1740.[2]

14

Photo of the village, 2011

Photo of the village, around 1900;
kindly loaned by Mr J.F. Williams, Cerrigydrudion.

This map produced in 1573 by Humphrey Lloyd which gives an idea of people's view of Wales at that time.[4]

nearly half were children and young people. On the whole, people lived in the scattered farms and small houses around the village with only a few properties, along with St Mary Magdalen's church and the two alehouses, clustered around the centre of the village, still known as the Llan.

By 1700, the population had only grown slightly and there were few extra properties, but by 1750 we begin to see quite a few changes. Baron Price had donated money for the Almshouse opposite the church which was to house 'six poor men' and quite a few more houses had been built around the Llan and along the roads leading out of the village, to house the rising population. Around the Llan were two or three shops, the blacksmiths and various other tradesmen's homes. Over the next fifty years the population began to rise more quickly, so that by 1812 it was over

1,000, which meant that more houses were needed and more shops were established as the range of goods available began to expand. The outlying communities of Cefn Brith, Pentrellyncymer and Cwmpenanner also began to grow and local businesses such as a new mill, another blacksmith and more weavers and tailors were established.

By 1812 Cerrigydrudion was one of the larger communities in North Wales with many travellers and visitors passing through on business or as part of the newly emerging tourist trade. As the population grew so more fairs and sales were arranged making Cerrigydrudion a popular centre for people from the surrounding neighbourhood. This book aims to give a detailed picture of the community between 1662-1812.

END NOTES

[1] Map computer generated by the Library, University of Aberystwyth.
[2] A more detailed map of the village around 1740.
[3] Photo of the village. 2010. taken by Myrddin ap Dafydd. Photo of the village around 1900. kindly loaned by Mr. J.F. Williams, Cerrigydrudion.
[4] Map produced by Mr. Humphrey Lloyd in 1573.

Chapter 2

HOW THE VILLAGE WAS ORGANISED

By the mid-seventeen hundreds a system had evolved which met the needs of the small scattered communities that existed throughout the British Isles. Each area was divided into a parish with the boundaries usually being natural features such as hills and rivers. Each parish had a church, many dating back centuries, such as St Marys, Betws Gwerfyl Goch, built in the late twelfth century, and others founded much earlier and then replaced with a permanent, stone building rather than the wooden structures which had been erected in the beginning. According to the church records for St Mary Magdalen church in Cerrigydruion, it was founded in 440AD by the followers of St Patrick. The present stone building dates from the late fifteenth century.[1] The map shows the parishes around Cerrigydrudion and, it can be seen that a small area between Ysbyty Ifan and Cerrigydrudion which is now known as Pentrefoelas and Rhydlydan was then a separate part of Llannefydd Parish.[2]

Everyone knew which parish they lived in and the legal rights that went with this. People had the right to live and work within the parish, to claim financial help from the parish if they fell on hard times, to be baptised, married and buried in the Parish Church and, with permission from the Justice of the Peace, to build a new house or extend an existing property.

Parish Officials[3] were elected at a meeting held annually, usually on Easter Monday. This meeting was held in the local Alehouse and was known as the Vestry Meeting. The Rector and any curates attended along with householders from the parish. All the parish officers were elected for a year and, as far as

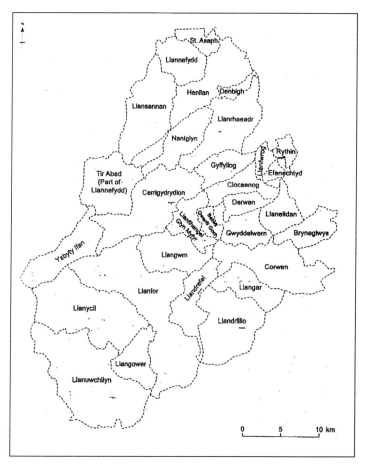

Map of Parishes

19

possible, represented the different areas of the parish. With the exception of the Parish Clerk, all officers were unpaid, although some travelling expenses seem to have been given.

Two churchwardens were appointed, one by the Rector and the other by the Vestry Meeting. Their duties included keeping

order in the church and churchyard and ensuring that the church was clean and provided with a font, reading desk, altar and bells. Every church was meant to have a chest to keep the chalice and patten needed for communion, along with the necessary linen and the Rector's white surplice and the register of baptisms, marriages and burials were all kept.

The chest in Betws Gwerfyl Goch Church.[4]

They also had to provide the bread and wine ready for the monthly communion services. Each chest was meant to have three keys, one held by the Rector and the other two were held by the wardens.. They also had to make sure that the tools for burials, such as spades, a wooden coffin and a suitable cloth, were in good order. The wardens kept accounts which were presented annually at the Vestry and, although no records survive for Cerrigydrudion, neighbouring parishes show expenditure on Bibles, Prayer Books, candles, bread and wine, as well as repairs to the bells, the mending of the thatched roof and, in the early 1730s. the flagging of the church floor with stone. The roof of

Cerrigydrudion church was slated about 1800. Until 1760 the Churchwardens also served as Overseers of the Poor, but with the growth in the population in Cerrigydrudion two separate people were appointed. The work involved included the care of the poor throughout the parish. Money was raised through a levy on the parishioners and with donations in the Poor Box found in every church especially on Sacrament Sunday. They were to provide housing for the poor, care for the sick, the elderly and orphaned children, and to supply work apprenticeships for those able to work. The idle and workshy could be sent to the House of Correction in Ruthin. They were also responsible for making sure people lived within their own parishes

By the 1790s, as the population grew, the pressure on their funds meant that they were more vigilant about returning people to their own parish if they were likely to be an expense on the parish. Occasionally, if there was no one who could pay for the funeral of someone who had died, the Overseers would arrange this. Because there was a considerable amount of paperwork the Overseers tended to be well-educated and able to deal with legal matters if they arose. The records kept by the Overseers from Bryneglwys[5] show that money was spent on practical things such as potatoes to plant, as well as clothes and shoes.

The roads during this period were little more than rough tracks, often very rutted and muddy with grass growing on them. It was the responsibility of each householder to maintain the roads bordering their properties, which was a difficult and thankless task.The vestry appointed people as Surveyors of the Highways. Their job was to inspect the roads and ensure that householders turned out during the summer to clear and tidy the roads. In 1798 Jane Roberts and her son from Pant y Griafolen were taken to court and fined for failing to maintain their stretch of road.

The Constable was also appointed by the Vestry to check for example, that the miller was not giving short weight or the shoemaker using inferior materials. Again this was not a popular office because people saw the Constable as interfering with their lives. As well as keeping watch on tradesmen, he also dealt with petty crimes. John Cadwaladr of Pentre Cwm, who died in 1702, is the only person mentioned as a Constable, although there were obviously others.

If the offence was more serious the Constable would refer it on to the Justice of the Peace. These men were appointed by the Crown. They would deal with most problems by issuing either a warning or a fine. More serious matters would be taken to the Denbighshire Quarter Sessions which met in either Denbigh or Ruthin. These cases were recorded and then kept in rolls. A number of clergy served as Justices of the Peace, including in the 1760s Humphrey Humphreys and in the 1790s James Price.

The Parish Clerk[6] was appointed by the Vestry and recorded the minutes of that meeting as well as keeping the church register. He was paid a small sum for recording baptisms, weddings and burials and had to send an annual list to the Bishop of St Asaph. He was often called on by parishioners to help with legal matters, to write or witness wills and as a witness at weddings. Parish Clerks tended to stay in office for some years.

On the whole, this system worked well. Communities were small enough for people to know one another and the work load was not too onerous. However, by the beginning of the nineteenth century some villages, including Cerrigydrudion, had grown considerably and this was putting a lot of pressure on the Overseers of the Poor who had limited financial resources to help the growing number needing help.

A number of people left money in their wills to help the poor. The

Benefactors' Board in the church lists some of these.[7]

Thomas Parry of Pentre Cwm who died in 1684 left £100, with the interest to be used each year to help the poor. The records are available from 1709 and list the people given money and the amounts. All widows were helped, at least when they were first widowed. and some widowers, especially those with a number of children. In 1738 Mary Waring, wife of Edward Jones of Ty Tan y Mynwent, died four days after giving birth to her sixth child. The charity gave Edward Jones 7s-0d that year and a smaller amount for a number of years afterwards.

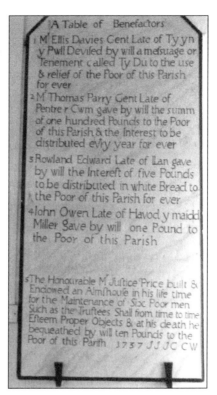

The Benefactors' Board.

Money was given to those who were ill with 1s-0d given to Jane Williams' child *'being sick'* in 1711 and in the same year Cadwaladr Morris received 2s-0d for his children, his wife being sick from 1742 onwards. Alice of Swch received money for *'her lame lad.'* The Trustees were careful that the money was given to the *'deserving poor'* questioning in 1745 whether Cadwaladr Owen's son was *'not old enough to get his bread'*. Although it has not been possible to identify him further, Richard Thomas was given 4s-0d in 1714 'being in prison'. Families were meant to help support their relatives in prison.

David Vaughan from Cwm was married to Mary Jones on 5 July 1674. Although they had four children, sadly, they all died between 1710 and 1723, meaning that the couple had no family to support them as they grew older. David Vaughan was given money in 1741 and moved into the Almshouse where he died in 1746. Because there are no surviving records of the Overseers of the Poor these records give a valuable insight into who the poor were and how they were helped.

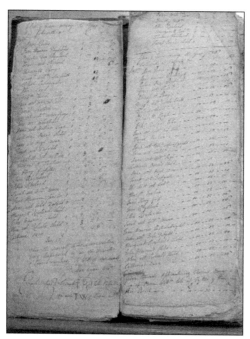

*A page from the
Thomas Parry Charity Records.*[8]

The money was usually given out on March 25th at a meeting attended by the Rector, the Curate, the Churchwardens and the Overseers of the Poor.

The book also contains details of five other legacies. In 1730 Sir William Middleton of Chirk Castle left £3 to the poor who received 2s-0d each. David Jones of the parish of

Llanfawr (Llanfor) left £3 in his will of 1760, Edward Evans of Tai Uchaf left £2-1s-0d to be distributed in 1774 and Ellis Jones who died in 1776 from Bryngwyn left 15s-0d. The names of the recipients and the amounts are all listed and are basically the same people as those receiving money from the Thomas Parry Charity and, so one can assume, the list used by the Overseers of the Poor.

Baron Price.[9]

Baron Price left £20 in his will of 1735 which was distributed in varying amounts from 2s-6d – 6s-0d.

As well as this charity Baron Price had already given money to build an Almshouse opposite the church. This was erected in 1717 and was intended to house 'six poor men'. The property consisted of one room with a garden at the back and a ty bach (toilet) at the end. During the latter part of the seventeenth and the eighteenth century many wealthy individuals or families gave money towards the building of Almshouses. In this area there were some on the Rhug Estate in Corwen, in Ysbyty Ifan, Llanrwst and Ruthin for example.

Robert, Baron Price, was the eldest son of Thomas Price, Geeler, and Margaret Wynne, Bwlch y Beudy, who were married

The Almshouse at the end of the nineteenth century.[10]

The Almshouse today

in 1650. This marriage united the two leading gentry families in the community. Gentry families in Wales were not necessarily very wealthy, but could trace their ancestors back to one of the fifteen great tribes of Wales. In the case of the Prices this was the tribe of Marchweithian who had links with families both in Pentrefoelas and Ysbyty Ifan, where there are three marble efigies in the church. Thomas Price and Margaret Wynne had eight children in total. The three boys went to London where two became freemen and citizens of London and the five girls all married into local gentry families, Ucheldre in Corwen, Maenan outside Llanrwst, Maysmore between Cerrigydrudion and Corwen, Garthmeilio in Llangwm and Plas Yffa in Llansannan. Thomas Price died young and his wife remained in the area even after her children had moved away. Robert kept close links with the area coming from London on a regular basis. He married an heiress from Herefordshire and became the Member of Parliament for Weobly, as well as serving as a legal officer both in Herefordshire and south Wales, before becoming a Judge in London. The Price family had built a chapel onto the south side of Cerrigydrudion Church during the latter part of the seventeenth century and there are memorial stones to both Thomas Price and Margaret Wynne there. The 1749 Terrier (a record of the church and its property) records that *'at the south east end of the church is a chapel erected by the ancestors of Uvedale Price Esq., being repaired by him as his property and having his ancestors buried there. The Almshouse residents usually sit there'.*[11] Uvedale was Robert Price's son.

The Almshouse was built in 1717 and land left by Robert Price in both Denbigh and Denbigh Green brought in an income to maintain the property and provide care for the residents. Each year they were given a great coat, stockings and shoes as well as a sum of money to be collected after Evensong at Christmas, Easter, St Mary Magdalen (22 July) and Michaelmas (29 September). They also wore a metal badge on their arm over their coat.

Baron Price was clearly a devout man who wanted to leave a

The metal badge worn by the Almshouse people.[12]

The plaque on the front of the Almshouse shows the family crest of Baron Price and the two Biblical quotations are about caring for the poor.[13]

lasting gift to help the poor. He also left money for an Almshouse in Hertfordshire although, unlike in Cerrigydrudion, it is now a private house.

The Diocese of St Asaph, in common with all Dioceses administered many legal matters from its centre in St Asaph. They issued licenses for clergy to minister in parish, for parish clerks and for midwives, who were meant to have some training, although it is difficult to know any details about this.

At the end of each year the Parish Clerk had to send a copy of the parish register listing all baptisms, marriages and burials.[14] We need to remember that this was the only record of these events during this period. If a couple were going to get married by Licence then they first had to see a surrogate, a clergyman licensed by the Diocese to apply for a Licence. Having filled in the details, this form was then delivered to the Legal Officer in St Asaph who would issue a Licence.

The Diocese also had to deal with all legal matters relating to someone's death. If the person had left a will, then this had to be validated before any action could take place. If the person who had died had not left a will then the family would apply for a Bond, which was a legal permission to sort out the person's estate. The majority of people did not make a will as it was clear who would inherit and many people had little or nothing to leave.

This pattern of local government worked well in small communities where there were enough capable people to hold the offices of churchwarden, overseer of the poor, constable, surveyor of the highways and parish clerk. Until the 1770s there were very few parishes in north Wales with more than 600 residents, but the next thirty years saw a rise in the population across the British Isles, due to a slow improvement n nutrition and housing. By 1800 many parishes were finding it difficult to provide for the poor, but it was not until 1834 that the Parliament passed the Poor Law Act which introduced new measures to help the poor.

The role of the Constable developed during the 1800s into a full-time Police Force with a local Constable in each community. The Surveyors of the Highways continued but, again became a full-time role organised by Denbighshire County Council. The Parish Clerk has become the Secretary to the Community Council, but no longer has the legal task of registering births, marriages and deaths, which is now done by a Registrar in each area.

The Churchwardens are still officers within the church with similar responsibilities within the church for maintenance of the church building and churchyard and are still appointed annually, one by the Rector and one by the congregation.

END NOTES

1   DRO. The Parish register for Cerrigydrudion begins in 1590.
2   DRO. This map is taken from early maps of the Diocese.
3   Details from 'The Compleat Parish Officer.' Originally published in 1734. Facsimilie copy produced by The Wiltshire Family History Society in 1994.
4   Drawn by Mrs Biddy Greenwood. 2000.
5   DRO. PD/11/1/22-24. Records of the Overseers of the Poor.
6   See the chapter on Meet the People for further information.
7   Photo of the Benefactors' Board taken by Myrddin ap Dafydd.
8   DRO. Thomas Parry Charity Records.
9   NLW. This picture is taken from the short biography of Baron Price written by Richard Currill.
10   Photo of the Almshouse taken around 1900. Kindly loaned by Mr. J.F.Williams, Cerrigydrudion.
11   NLW. Terrier for Cerrigydrudion. 1749.
12   DRO. The badges are with the Baron Price collection.
13   Photo of the crest on the front of the Almshouses taken by Myrddin ap Dafydd.
14   NLW. These are known as the Bishop's Transcript.

Chapter 3

BIRTH, MARRIAGE AND DEATH

Life in rural north Wales in the eighteenth century followed a fairly predictable pattern. Children were born at home, usually with the help of a midwife, and were brought up to work on the farm, around the house and with the business. By the age of twelve or thirteen most girls would have been placed 'in service' working on other farms and helping around the house, boys would also be employed on farms or be apprenticed to a trade such as tailoring or weaving. Wealthier families may have employed a governess to educate their children and boys would have been sent to a Grammar School such as Llanrwst, Ruthin or Denbigh and maybe on to University in Oxford or Cambridge.

The majority of people did not get married until their middle twenties and, having found a house, probably stayed there for many years raising four or five children. Nearly all households consisted of just two generations known as a 'nuclear' family. There was, of course, no pension provision, and so most people continued to work, although families and the Overseers of the Poor would help those who became too elderly or infirm to work to work.

Nearly everybody died at home with family and friends around them and the Rector calling to visit. They were buried after a service in Church within their own community.

Almost every baby was baptised, with the exception of the children of Quakers who did not believe in baptism. The only record of a baby's existence was the record in the church register as public registration of births, marriages and deaths did not come in until the 1834.

This chart shows the number of babies baptised in Cerrigydrudion between 1660 – 1812.

Date	Girls	Boys	Total
1660 – 69	106	89	195
79	101	100	201
89	95	98	193
99	105	105	210
1700 – 09	107	130	237
19	69	116	185
29	110	104	214
39	126	120	246
49	121	159	280
59	124	152	276
69	138	124	262
79	144	178	322
89	156	170	326
99	146	153	299
1800 – 09	137	152	262
1810 – 12	58	44	102
	1843	1974	3817

As can be seen, more boys were baptised than girls but the record show that more boys died as babies than girls and so the numbers almost equal out. It is also possible to see the slow growth in numbers which is shown in the expansion in the population between 1662 – 1812.

The early church records which were written in Latin, give very little information about the child other than it's name and the name of the father, but by the 1670s the mother's name was

A page from the Register.
1590-1735.[1]

included and usually the house name, making it fairly straightforward to identify families.

The Book of Common Prayer stated that *'it is most convenient that Baptism should not be administered but upon Sundays and other Holy Days.'* However, most babies were baptised within two or three days of their birth with a service in church taken by the Rector. The father and godparents would take the child as the mother would still be recovering from childbirth. A few babies had their baptism delayed for up to ten days, one reason for this may have been the weather, for example, David, the son of Hugh David and Mary, who lived five miles from the church in Pentrellyncymer, was baptised on 16 November 1690 a week after he was born. Illegitimate children were often baptised later as the father may not have been available to take the child to church. John, the illegitimate son of William John and Alice John was baptised thirteen days after he was born on 2 April 1694. Some gentry families also delayed the baptism; perhaps because they wanted more distant relatives to attend, and also to provide food for a celebration. Margaret and Peter, the children of Peter Morris and Gwen, of Hafod y Maidd waited almost a week before their children were baptised in 1690 and 1693 respectively. There were probably a few families, as well, who were not very organised or bothered.

The Rector would have made the arrangements for the service, with clean water in the font and, as well as his black cassock, he would have worn a white surplice.. During the service promises were made by the father and godparents to bring up the child in the Christian faith and then the Rector would put water on the baby's head and maybe the sign of the cross, baptising the baby by name. After the service everyone would go to the Alehouse to celebrate. There were two alehouses opposite the church so there was plenty of choice! It is difficult to identify godparents because they are not listed in the Registers with one exception. On 18 October 1706 Philip Jones was baptised. He was the illegitimate son of Thomas Jethhood of Whitchurch (Denbigh) and Martha Jones of Cwmoerddwr. The godparents are named as Meredith Williams and Owen Jones. Meredith Williams was a near neighbour and Owen Jones was the baby's uncle. A number of wills, however, mention gifts being left to godchildren and godparents. Ales Burchinshaw,[2] of Llaethwryd, left her goddaughter, Elizabeth, a feather bed and bolster in 1694, Hugh Davies, of Bryngwyn,[3] left his godmother a feather bed and a large chest for keeping oatmeal in 1717 and in 1789 William David,[4] of Penybryn left his godson, Robert Edwards, 10s. Some people would have asked wealthier neighbours in the hope that they would help out with the child.

The mother of the baby was not expected to go out until she had recovered from childbirth, which could take up to a month, and then her first journey would be to church. After the usual service she would come forward to the front and the Rector would offer prayers of thanksgiving for the safe delivery of the baby. This service, found in the Book of Common Prayer was known as 'Churching'. It opened with the words *'forasmuch as it has pleased Almighty God of his goodness to give you safe delivery, and hath preserved you in the great danger of childbirth, you shall therefore give hearty thanks to Almighty God'* A psalm was said followed by the Lord's Prayer and the short service concluded with other prayers for the family.

It has been assumed that many women died in childbirth, but this was not actually the case. There was always an anxiety that the mother would die, but in reality most women survived. What is noticeable, however, is that a considerable number of women

35

only had one child, which may well indicate that the birth was a difficult one, possibly not helped by the primitive instruments used by midwives. Most villages would have had a midwife. They did not have any formal training and were usually widows who could earn some income to support themselves and any family that they had. All midwives were meant to be licensed by the Diocese and provided with a manual to help them. In an emergency they could also baptise a baby if the Rector was unavailable to reach the house in time.

Because most people married in their mid to late twenties they usually had four to five children in all. The few families who had more than nine children all married before they were twenty and often lived miserable lives moving from house to house with no settled employment or income.

The children, especially the girls, from gentry families were expected to get married at a young age, with marriages arranged so that land and businesses could be united. On the whole, however, people seem to have been able to choose their partners and stayed with them for life.

It is interesting to note that of the 3,817 babies baptised between 1662 – 1812 there were only 46 pairs of twins. Eleven were girls, twenty one were boys and fourteen one of each. The death rate for twins was noticeably higher. We need to remember that most people would not have known that they were expecting twins and one child may well have been much weaker than the other, or born prematurely, putting the babies at greater risk.

The most popular names were:

Jane	325	John	332
Margaret	232	Robert	304
Elizabeth	197	William	185
Catherine	186	Thomas	162
Ellin	147	David	157
Anne	131	Evan	135
Mary	113		

Cerrigydrudion Church is dedicated to St Mary Magdalen and it is noticeable that Magdalen is quite a popular name. Quite a number of Welsh names occur including Ellis, Cadwaladr, Meredith, Gaynor, Gwen and Lowry and towards the turn of the nineteenth century the rise in popularity of Biblical names such as Moses and Aaron. A few names seem to run in families with the name Gawen appering through three generations of the family at Ty Isa, Cwm and Daniel in the family from Hafod Elwy.

Nearly all children were born to parents who were married to each other. Illegitimacy rates were very low throughout the British Isles during the eighteenth century and only show a slow rise at the beginning of the nineteenth century. These children were named differently, being given their own name and then the name of their mother's father[5]. They were rarely given family names and were often given quite unusual names like Ffoulk and Charity. The church registers identify these children as being 'illegitimate' or 'base' but, nearly always include the father's name as he was expected to pay maintenance of around 6d a week. If the child could not be provided for by the father then the Overseers of the Poor would have to do this. The Denbigh Session Rolls show court cases that took place to establish paternity. On 11 February 1740 Margaret Lloyd of Cerrigydrudion was examined 'to name her illegitimate child's father'.[5] She named,

Edward Jones of Hendre, Llangwm. A week later he was summoned to appear before the next Quarter Sessions for fathering an illegitimate child. It would appear that the Court Cases took place before the baby was born as the church register records the child's baptism as taking place on 25 April 1740. Margaret Jones is described as 'the concubine of Edward Jones'.

Some fathers left money in their wills for their illegitimate children The wealthy David Davies,[6] of Llaethwryd left £4 to his son Thomas, and Charles Rowlands,[7] an inkeeper from Ceirnioge left '£200 at interest to maintain his son until he is 21'.

The register also records the sad case of two sisters Elin and Margaret. Both had a child in 1711 fathered by John Edward, a farm worker from Llanrhaeadr. Margaret's baby, Thomas, was baptised on 3 October and Margaret died at the end of January Meanwhile Elin's daughter, Catherine, was baptised on 22 November and died a week later, leaving Elin to look after Thomas, her nephew.

Jonet Robert is the only woman recorded in the register as having had two illegitimate children, and in neither case is the father named. Robert Lloyd, described as a 'gentleman' from Hafod y Maidd, fathered four children between 1797 – 1807. All four mothers were described as 'maids'.

During the eighteenth century Cerrigydrudion became a busy centre for trade and a number of the fathers of illegitimate children came from comunities quite a distance away. Some illegitimate children were accepted into the family and inherited land and farms. Charles Einion the son of Einion Thomas and Jonet Evans took his father's name and lived with his family in Pentre Cwm after his birth in 1699 By 1742 he was married to Jane and settled at Pentre Cwm where they had four children.

Although nearly all children were born in wedlock a

considerable number of women were pregnant when they got married. About 10% had a baby within eight months of their marriage. The couples came from all sorts of backgrounds. Edward Jones and Elizabeth, both from gentry families were married on 17 May 1766 when Elizabeth was three months pregnant. Robert Lewis, a farm labourer and Margaret, who were also married in 1766, had a baby one month after their wedding.[8]

Most novels written during this period, such as those by Jane Austen, focus on better off families where the girls were expected to be married by their early twenties, but the vast majority of people married when they were older, in Cerrigydrudion men were about twenty seven and women twenty five. Neighbouring parishes all show a similar pattern. By this time the couple would have been able to save some money and collect together most of the things they would need to set up house. A number of wills show that bedding and furniture were left to children to help gather together the basics they needed. The four grandchildren of Mary Vaughan from Bwlch were left 'all her bedding',[9] William Thomas of Capelle left *'1 feather bed, 1 bedstead and 2 pairs of sheets'*[10] for his daughter, Jane, and Gethin Lloyd from Clust y Blaidd left his wife Jane, *'1 pair of sheets, 2 pairs of blankets and a coverlet which she had brought with her when she married.'*[11]

About 10% of couples began married life living with parents or in-laws. This may have meant sharing a house or living in a small extension built on the end of a family home. Wiliam Prichard and Jane David lived with Jane's parents at Bwlch y Beudy until the birth of their first child in 1711 when they moved to Hendre Bach.

Before the wedding invitations, often verbal, were sent out and small presents were given. Gloves were very popular, as were carved love spoons and knitting sheaths,

39

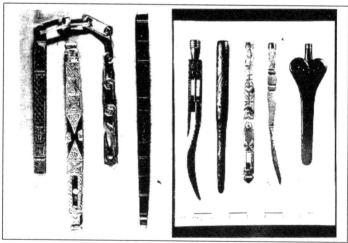

Love spoons and knitting sheaths.[12]

which were put into the waistband to hold one needle so that people could do other things at the same time. In a dominantly farming community most couples got married during the winter months when there was less work to do. Rents on land and property were due at Michaelmas (September 29) and so people started to rent a property after then. Traditionally the church taught that people should not get married during the two penetential seasons of the church's year, Advent, which is the four weeks before Christmas and Lent, the six weeks before Easter. On the whole people seem to have observed this with only twenty-six weddings in Advent and nineteen in Lent during the years 1662 – 1812.

Weddings had to be conducted in church and could take place eiher after the Banns had been called in church or a Licence issued. The Rector read out the following statement for three consecutive Sundays and, if there were no objections, the marriage could go ahead. *'I publish the Banns of Marriage between [name], bachelor of [name of parish] and [name], spinster of [name of parish]. This is for the first [second, third] time of asking. If ye know cause or just impediment why this couple should not be joined together in Holy Matrimony ye are to declare it'*. Some people, usually the better off, chose to get married by Licence. This involved making a legal declaration and receiving a cerificate of permission from the Bishop's legal officer. Being married by Licence cost 5s – 7s, more than being married by Banns.

The law of the land stated that there were a number of classes of people who could not marry one another. For example, a son could not marry his mother and a girl could not marry her uncle. The list, known as the 'The Table of Kindred and Affinity' was meant to be displayed in each church and read out twice a year at the end of a service. The intention being to prevent marriage between close relatives.

The marriage service in The Book of Common Prayer began with a reading from St John chapter 2 telling the story of Jesus at the marriage in Cana and continued with a summary of the importance of marriage. The vows were then exchanged and the ring placed on the woman's finger. The Rector then prayed for God's blessing on the couple and finished with prayers for them as they began their married life together. Legally, there had to be two witnesses at the wedding, although there would usually have been many more with family and friends.

Quite a number of wills show the affection felt by husbands towards their wives. John Lawrence[13] left money to his children and 'his loving wife Ellin' and John Hughes of Bwlch y Beudy's will included these words 'to my loving and most dear wife, as a small recompense for her affectionate tenderness and care of me.'[14] No doubt some marriages were not so happy, but most couples seem to have stayed together, divorce not being an option.

Although marriage in church was the only legal way to get married some people abused the system taking supposed weddings in alehouses and other public places. Some clergy were also guilty of taking 'clandestine' marriages! This was possible if the couple got married by Licence without any questons being asked. Lewis Lewis, the Rector of Betws Gwerfyl Goch between 1743 – 1754 took fifty six weddings during this time, with forty five being by Licence. The register shows that nearly all these people came from outside the parish including one from Coventry and one from 'Leverpool' as well as Abergele, Llangynog and Ruthin. He was paid quite well for this, improving his income considerably. Other clergy from the parishes of Bryneglwys, Carrog and Gwyddelwern were also reported to the Bishop for this practice. In 1749 The Rural Dean wrote to the Bishop saying that when he had stopped the Rector of Gwyddelwern from taking clandestine marriages a layman had taken over. He wrote *'I prosecuted the layman for so doing and obtained an order from the Justice of the Peace at the Quarter Sessions in Bala to have him whipt there in the public market which not only terrified him but all others from being guilty.'* [15]

In 1753 Hardwicke's Marriage Act was finally passed in Parliament standardising marriage practices and clarifying the regulations. A new printed Register was issued to each church which listed the date, the couples' names and marital status, whether they were married by Banns or Licence, the names of the witnesses and who took the service. All had to sign or make their mark. This was intended to stop couples getting married when they were under the age of 21 without their parents consent, to prevent bigamous marriages and to offer some protection against forced marriages.

It was inevitabe that some couples had their marriages curtailed by the death of one partner and the registers show that some widowers remarried quite quickly. This may have been partly for practical reasons, if they were left with young children to bring up for example. Robert David of Ty'n Braich married Jane Middleton nine months after his wife had died in 1746. James Price, the Rector of Cerrigydrudion's first wife was buried around 1791 leaving him with three young daughters he remarried in 1793, at the age of thirty-six, and had two more daughters. Sadly, his second wife died in June 1801.

Owen Owen married four times, his first wife, Mary Davies, was a widow who owned Plas Onn. Property laws in this period stated that a woman's property passed to the ownership of her husband when she got married. Mary Davies died in January

Marriage Register [16]

1798 and Owen Owen continued to live in Plas Onn where in August 1799 he brought his new wife Dorothy Williams, who was eight months pregnant. She died in 1800. By March 1803 he had married Margaret Ellis, who was six months pregnant and who died in April 1805. At the end of 1806 he married Sarah Edwards who was also pregnant when they were married!

It is difficult to know how long marriages lasted, but from over 1,000 recorded weddings it was possible to find fifty-five couples where both the date of their wedding and the date of one partners' funeral was recorded.

3 marriages lsted less than 1 year
4 lasted 1 – 5 years
6 lasted 6 – 10 years
4 lasted 11 – 15 years
8 lasted 16 – 20 years
11 lasted 21 – 25 years
2 lasted 26 – 30 years
5 lasted 31 – 35 years
5 lasted 36 – 40 years
7 lasted more than 40 years

Those over forty years were 43, 44, 45, 48, 52 54 and 55. The average length was 21-25 years but it is impossible to know if this is representative . Two of the very long marriages are from the same family. Edward Cadwaladr and Magdalen David were married on 17 June 1708 and lived in Ty Coch. They were married for fifty-five years. Their son Edward Cadwaladr was married on 11 September 1736 to Gwen Thomas and lived in Hendre Bach. They were married for fifty-three years. Two of the three marriages that ended in less than a year appear to have been due to the wife's death in childbirth.

Most people married someone who lived nearby, if not in the same parish or a neighbouring one. Of the 669 marriages where the register records where the couple came from, both partners came from Cerrigydrudion in 301 cases and 368 show that one partner came from a neighbouring parish within a five mile radius. The few weddings when one partner, always the man came from further afield show the woman as living in the Llan where the shops and alehouses were and where travellers stopped overnight or came to sell their wholesale goods in the shops. Owen Thomas, a widower from Amlwch, married Jane Thomas on 16 July 1788. When their first child was born Owen is described as a shopkeeper. Amlwch on Anglesey was an important commercial centre by the middle of eighteenth century.

It is estimated that about 80% of the whole population got married. There were certainly plenty of single people in Cerrigydrudion during the eighteenth century. Some women would have remained at home to look after elderly or sick parents or perhaps younger children. Others, both men and women, settled as servants and farm labourers within a family and had a valued role there. Presumably, some people did not meet the right partner, or one partner died before they could be married. Others lived independantly, perhaps with a maid to help them. A few women, who had some money, were able to make a living by lending out money at interest. The inventories of two women show this, Margaret Thomas, who died in 1711 was 'aged and weak'. Her inventory included *'all money due by specially £15.'*[17] Martha Williams, 'an old, maiden lady' had money at interest £7 10s 0d, listed in her inventory.[18] The wills of some single people show their continued links with family and friends. Edward Griffith, a yeoman from Hafod y Maidd, who died in 1693, left sums of money to his nephews and nieces varying in amounts from £60- £1.[19] Morris Williams of Geeler who died in 1775, left his nephew £3, his niece 12 lb of coarse wool, his sister, Jane, £2 and the remainder of his estate to his other sister, Elizabeth.[20] Besides nephews and nieces, William David, of Pen y Bryn who died in 1789 left 10s to Edward Hughes, 'a relation', 'my Bible to Gwen Morgan of Betws y Coed, 10s to Robert Edwards, his godson, and his three piece oak cupboard to Margaret Owen 'an old maid'.[21]

In the eighteenth century almost everyone died at home, usually with family and friends around them. Very few people would have reached adulthood without death touching their lives, children experienced the death of brothers and sisters, grand-parents and sometimes their own parents, as well as neighbours and friends. Many would have echoed the words of the Rev. William Hughes, Rector of Llanfihangel Glyn Myfyr, written at the beginning of his will in 1755, *'Minding the uncertainty of this life and the certainty of that to come, I commend my soul to Almighty God.'*[22]

It is a commonly held view that people in this period died young and it is certainly true that a large number of babies and small children did die, but if people passed the age of ten, then they had a good chance of living a long life. The Rector of Cerrigydruidon took on average of eighteen funerals a year of which about six (one third) were children under the age of ten, the majority being small babies.

However, two thirds of people lived into adulthood and a good number into their seventies and eighties. Evidence from neighbouring parishes shows the same pattern, with people living into their nineties and one person from Llansannan who died when they were 102.

Hardly any of the parish registers give an indication of the cause of death unless it was an accident. These included people who drowned, were hit by carts and occasional vagrants found dead under hedges or in barns. Medical knowledge was fairly limited and as people got older it was assumed that they would die of 'old age'. The registers of Llanrhaeadr ym Mochnant are an exception to this. During the period from 1759-1808 when Rev'd Dr William Worthington was Rector the cause of death was listed and this practice continued for over fifty years. These causes have been analysed and clarified by Dr E. J. J. Davies, of Cerrigydrudion, in a fascinating article. 1,675 deaths were recorded during that time and by far the largest number,606, (37.4%) died of decay, 254 (15.5%) died of a fever and 182 (11.1%) of old age. 110 (6.7%) died of smallpox amd the remainder of palsy, chincough. dropsy, consumption, convulsions and cholick. 25 women (1.5%) died in chilbirth, which follows the same pattern as that in Cerrigydrudion and elsewhere.[21]

People who became ill and died at home after a period of time were able to sort out their affairs. The Rector woud have visited them and taken a service of Prayers for the Sick which encouraged people to put things right with their family, neighbours and friends and to make a will. There are eighty wills available, which were made between 1700 – 1812, of these:

10 were made less than a week before the person died
20 within a month
15 within 2 – 6 months
3 within 7 – 12 months
8 within 1 year
12 within 2 – 3 years
10 within 4 – 8 years
1 within 11 years
1 within 12 years

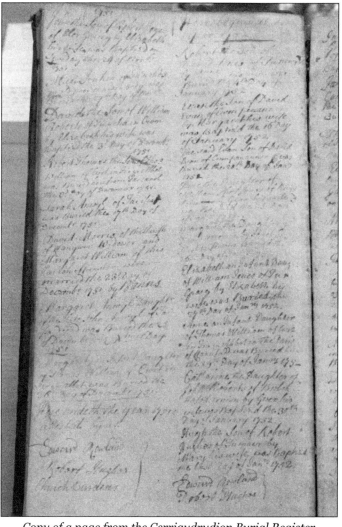

Copy of a page from the Cerrigydrudion Burial Register
1735-1812.[24]

Most wills begin by affirming that the person was sick or weak in body but sound in mind. Morris Evans of Fron Isa made his will on 23 April 1750 and was buried two days later. Some people seem to have made their will when they were ill and then recovered and lived a few years longer. Evan Davies of Bwlch y Beudy made his will on 1 June 1753, probably when he handed over his estate to his son, Robert. Evan died in 1760.

25

Picture of the will of Evan Davies.[25]

This is an interesting will, written by the Rector, Evan Wynne, in 1753. the witnesses were Evan Wynne, his wife Rebecca Wynne (it was very unusual for a woman to witness a will) and Lewis Lloyd, the Parish Clerk. In the will he leaves 'money for gloves'. These were probably leather gloves for the bearers to wear.

Although there were professional undertakers in London and other large towns, families in rural areas still organised the funeral temselves. Churches owned the tools, coffin and cloths needed to dig the grave and to carry the person from home to the church. In 1729 Rev'd John Wynne, Rural Dean[26] wrote a detailed report of each church in his area. He wrote of the parish of Llanycil, *'their several implement for burial are perfect, they have two, strong shoulder biers and a horse litter for the carriage of their dead. They have, likewise a good burying cloath, a competent number of spades, a pick axe, and an iron bar, and in short, want nothing that is necessary or convenient excepting a hand bell'*. In contrast, Llangower, on the opposite side of the Lake, *'have one shoulder bier for funerals and a coarse, brownish, torn cloath to cover it. The clerk is forced to use his own spade to dig the graves, the parish allowing him none at all.'* At the beginning of the nineteenth century the churchwardens of Cerrigydrudion reported to the Bishop that they had everything they needed for a funeral. The body would have been kept at home until the day of the funeral, which would have been three to five days after the person had died. It would then have been carried to Church in the bier with family and friends following on.

For many centuries people had been buried in a linen shroud, but by the 1660s there was a growing lobby of sheep farmers who wanted shrouds to be made of wool. In 1678 Parliament passed a law agreeing to this, and stating that people burried in any other material would have to pay a fine. Inerestingly, there is a note in the Cerrigydrudion register after the burial of Catherine uch Robert of Elor Garreg on 1 October 1678 which reads, *'oath was made before Cadd'r Wynne of Voelas, Esq., one of His Majesty's Justices of the Peace for this country by two credible witnesses whose names are subscribed, that ye said catherine was wound and buried in no other shift or shroud, nor the coffin lined and fur'd (furnished) with any other cloth, stuff or material, than that which is made of sheep's wool only, according to an Act of Parliament in the case made and proved.'*

In an area with plenty of sheep this was a popular move and there are no records of people choosing to be buried in linen. In the parish of Hanmer, on the English/Welsh border, however, quite a number of gentry families are recorded as being buried in linen. The register records them as paying a fine of around £2 10s 0d to 'the poor of the parish'.

The coffin and mourners would be met at the church gate by the Rector. Quite a number of churches had gates with a roof and stone ledges to rest the coffin on, known as a lych gate. The service began with sentences from the Bible and contined in the church with Bible readings and prayers for the mourners before the person was comended to God. The theme was the hope of the resurrection and comfort for the mourners. The coffin was then carried to the graveside. Until the middle of the eighteenth century it appears that most people were then taken from the coffin and buried just in their shroud, although this practice became much less common by the turn of the nineteen century. However, it had been the custom for the gentry family members to be buried in the church. The will of David ap Price, yeoman, of Ty'n y Waen, who died in 1690 stated, *'I give and bequeath to the Church of Cerrigydrudion 30s, provided I am permitted to be buried under the said church.'*[27] Then a note was placed in the church register on 11 April 1696 which reads *'Memorandum that the corps of Maurice Annwyl of Tai yn y Voel was interred under the altar of the parish church of Cerrigydrudion by and with the consent of Mr. Robert Wynne, Rector of the parish, whose right it is. No one else to be buried under the allor.'* This was signed by five men including Lewis Annwyl the son of Maurice Annwyl. Some of the old plaques now on the wall of many churches including Cerrigydrudion were probably on the floor originally.

The practice of burying under the church floor was still taking place in Llanfihangel Glyn Myfyr as the Rector discovered, when he placed a seat for his family by the altar in 1754.A declaration written by him and witnessed by Hugh Cadwaladr on 11 October 1754.stated, *'I, David Davies, Rector of Llanfihangel G.M do own and acknowledge that the burying place under the seat that I have lately erected on ye north side of the altar belongs to David Jones of Galltvaynan and that he, or his tenants are at liberty at any time to take down the said.seat. As written by my hand ye day and year above written.'*[28]

Quite a number of churches had 'box pews', there are a number in Llangar Church, which is between Corwen and Cynwyd. These were originally placed in church by wealthy families who had to apply for permission from the Diocese to place a box pew. This meant that members of the family could be buried under the pew.

The practice of burying people within the church slowly stopped for a number of reasons. Firstly, because the church was full, secondly, because people began to feel that it was not hygienic and thirdly, because churches began to put flagstones onto their earth floors, which had been covered with rushes and the flagstones were more difficult to dig up. When wealthy families started to bury their loved ones outside they began to erect ornate tombstones and graves and some placed very large memorials on the walls inside the church. There is a good example in Cerrigydrudion church where Baron Price placed a stone memorial to his mother, Margaret, who died in 1723.

The Rector was paid for taking the funeral and the Parish Clerk received a small amount for recording the burial in the church register. There would be other costs including the shroud and ale for the mourners, after the service. Hugh David, a yeoman from Llanfihangel Glyn Myfyr left £3 in his will of 1713 to cover the cost of his funeral.[29]

One custom which seems to have been universal was the giving of money to buy gloves to be worn at the funeral both by the chief mourners and by the bearers. These would have been leather gloves made locally. The other universal custom was the ringing of bells. Almost every church had a belfry with at least one bell. This was rung when someone died to let the community know of the death and then to call people to the funeral as well as being rung on Sundays at service times.

Traditionally, unbaptised babies and people who committed suicide were not meant to be buried in the churchyard. If a sickly baby was born the midwife could baptise it if the Rector did not arrive in time. It seems that this rule was often waived with babies being buried with family members and people who had committed suicide having a service at night before being buried on the north side of the churchyard.

During the period 1662 – 1812, 320 babies were buried during the first month of their life out of a total of 3,817 recorded baptisms. An infant mortality rate of nearly 10%. After that the numbers dropped considerably with

95 dying between 2 – 6 months

35 dying between 7 – 12 months

Meaning that 450 babies died before their first birthday. Between the ages of 1 – 10 a further 159 died and 35 more between 11 – 20. No reasons are given for these deaths but the causes of death listed earlier are obviously the ones leading to the death of so many young children.

Wills show that parents had a great love for their children and tried to make provision for them while they were still young. David Davies of Llaethwryd a wealthy man who died in 1758, left £110 to *'my son, Robert Davies for his being placed out in boarding or his education as his trustees and Guardians shall nominate.'*[30] Griffith Robert, a shoemaker from Y Gro on the edge of Betws Gwerfyl Goch parish died leaving his poor children in need of care. The Trustees were to keep house for everyone of them until they be married or some other necessity be made for them.. He left his four younger children £20 each to be paid when they grew up.[31]

Sadly, many families did not have the resources to make any provision for their children if one parent died. The records of the Thomas Parry Charity show clearly money being distributed to widows and widowers and no doubt the Overseers of the Poor also made contributions, although they had limited resources.

Life for people in this period seems to have followed a farily predicable pattern, although they would always be living with the fear of death through an accident or in childbirth. Although a very scattered community geographically it was a close one with family, friends and neighbours around.

END NOTES

1 DRO. Cerrigydrudion Register. 1590-1735.
2 NLW. SA/1694/23.
3 NLW. SA/1717/5.
4 NLW.1787/12.
5 DRO. QSD/SR/124/37.
6 NLW. SA/1759/151.
7 NLW. SA/1802/19.

9   NLW. SA/1710/10.
10 NLW. SA/1725/11.
11 NLW. SA/1726/18.
12 From the Welsh Folk Museum, Cardiff.
13 NLW. SA/1750/15.
14 NLW. SA/1760/14.
15 NLW. Rural Dean's Report for Penllyn and Edeyrnion. 1749.
16 DRO. Cerrigydrudion Marriage Register. 1753-1812.
17 NLW. SA/1711/
18 NLW. SA/1752/15.
19 NLW. SA/1693/20.
20 NLW. SA/1775/13.
21 NLW. SA/1789/12.
22 NLW. SA/1755/16.
23 Article in The Denbighshire Transactions for 2008.
24 DRO. Cerrigydrudion Burial Register.
25 NLW. SA/ 1760/14.
26 NLW. Rural Dean's Report for Penllyn and Edeyrnion. 1729.
27 NLW. SA/1699/14.
28 DRO. A small piece of paper with the Llanfihangel papers.
29 NLW. SA/1713/102.
30 NLW. SA/1758/151.
31 NLW. SA/1808/83.

Chapter 4

FARMING AND FOOD

Throughout the British Isles the majority of people in the seventeenth and eighteenth centuries still lived in the countryside and made their living by farming. Cerrigydrudion was no exception. The land was (and still is) hilly and much of it over 1,000 feet (300m) with farms scattered along the valleys and houses built near springs. There were a number of large farms such as Clust y Blaidd, Hafod y Maidd, Llaethwryd and Elor Garreg, where yeoman farmers employed people to work the land and help with the stock and smaller, family farms such as Tyddyn Bychan, Bryn Du and Rhyd Loyw, where just the family were employed. People who did not earn their living from farming directly were still dependant on the produce of farming, such as millers, weavers, tailors and butchers. Many of these people would also have kept a few hens or geese and maybe a pig or cow for their own domestic use. John Evan,[1] a miller, who died in 1737 had four cows and a horse worth £7 and Cadwaladr John,[2] from Llysan in Llanfihangel Glyn Myfyr, who died in 1685, and was described as a shoemaker, had four horses, four milk cows, one heifer, two oxen, twenty yearling sheep and some poultry.

The raising of stock was less dependant on the weather than growing crops and the majority of farms had a good number of sheep and some cows. Jane David,[3] of Hendre Bach, who died in 1732, left six cows and two heifers worth £16, two oxen £7-10s four horses £7-10s and a large flock of sheep, worth £20. In contrast, Robert Richard,[4] who died in 1736, from Hafod y Maidd had twenty five cows worth £13, eleven steers £10, six oxen £13, eight steers £16, four bullocks and a heifer £12, twelve steers £16-

6s-0d, twelve calfs £10-16s, ten horses £15 and 278 sheep worth £15 as well as oatmeal valued at £11-10s-0d, corn in the ground £20 and old hay £4-10s-0d. This was by far the largest farm and employed a number of people to do all the work.

Cattle and sheep were not kept primarily to produce meat although steers and bullocks would have been killed at a fairly early age. Cows were kept for their milk and the by-products of butter, cheese, cream and buttermilk and sheep, firstly for their fleece, then for their manure and lastly for their meat. Evan Edward,[5] of Elor Garreg, who died in 1755 had 20lbs of wool worth £2-10s-0d and William ap Evan Lloyd,[6] of Hafod y Maidd had twenty four sheep valued £14-3s-0d and wool worth £3 when he died in 1691

Little was known about breeding animals, the main cattle breed was the Welsh Black, which was a smaller breed than those bred now. It was towards the end of the eighteenth century that people started to take an interest in improving the breeds of cattle and local farmers began to set up Agricultural Societies. The one for Penllyn and Edeyrnion was in existence by 1815 and helped to improve the quality of animals being bred and to develop Agricultural Shows.

As well as stock, some crops were grown. These were mostly oats which thrive in a cool, damp climate and some barley and rye. Oats are a useful crop as they provide food for humans and horses and, after they have been harvested, provide food for sheep to graze on.

In 1810 Walter Davies (Gwallter Mechain)[7] published a survey of farming practices in North Wales which encouraged people to grow a wider variety of crops including barley as well as oats and rye and emphasised the importance of growing vegetables stressing that the poor should be given plots of land to grow their own vegetables. He also suggested that farmers started to breed cattle more specifically for beef production and to develop better care for all stock. He included the average weights of a fleece which in the Cerrigydrudion area was 1 - 2lbs (now 4lb or 2kg. We need to remember that the lanolin is not washed, now and so there is more weight, and electric shears are used which produce more wool.)

Most people kept four to ten cows which were pastured outside for as much of the year as possible. Rather than being brought in for milking the cows were milked in the fields. The pails were then covered with a tightly fitting lid and carried back to the dairy, either by hand or hung on a yoke placed onto the person's shoulders.

A number of inventories list the items needed for milking and dairying generally. Jane David,[8] of Hendre Bach, who died in 1732 had a butter chest valued at 15S-0d and cheese press worth 4s-0d, both in 'the outchamber'. Evan Edwards,[9] who died in 1755, from Elor Garreg, a large farm, had;

1 churn	5s-6d
1 pail	1s-0d
1milk pail	6d
2 butter tubs with butter	14s-0d
1 buttermilk tub	3s-4d
1milk pail	1s-0d
and cows worth	£4

When Robert Richard died in 1736 his inventory from Hafod y Maidd listed twenty five cows for milking and a long list of the implements needed.

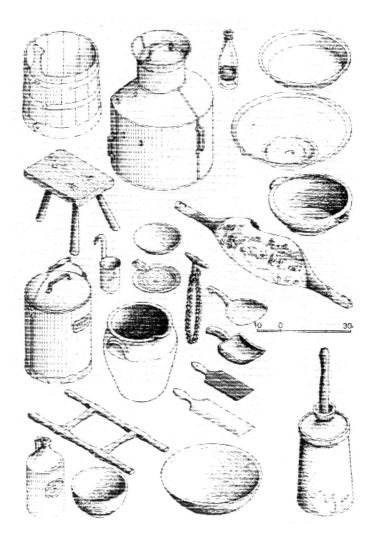

Drawings of various items used for butter and cheese making.[10]

Parcel of pails	4s-6d
2 tubbs	5s-6d
1 churn	7s-0d
2 pans	£3-0s-0d
2 pails	2s-0d
2 bowls	2s-0d
13 milking pails	18s-6d
1 tub	4s-0d

As well as a number of items for cheese making.

Some early inventories refer to 'pales' which were made by putting a series of pieces of wood around a base and pressing them tightly together with a metal ring. One piece of wood was longer than the others and used as a handle. Later, a piece of metal was fixed across the bucket in a way we are familiar with. Farms had sheds or barns, 'shippen' attached to them where cattle would be kept during the winter.

Until the 1750's most people used oxen to plough the fields and inventories show farms with two, four or six oxen and yokes to keep them together as a pair. However, this was a slow and cumbersome way to plough a field and most people were using horses by the end of the 1750s. A number of inventories list horses in groups as working horses and riding horses. Gethin Lloyd,[11] of Clust y Blaidd, who died in 1726 left '*1mare, 1 in fole mare, 1 mare an fole, 1 colt and one other mare valued at £17.*' Evan Edward,[12] from Elor Garreg, whose inventory was made in 1755 listed, '*1sorrel mare and filly, 1 black mare and filly, and 1 black colt worth £13-5s-0d.*' However, horses needed far more land to graze than oxen, cattle and sheep, and keeping horses cut down on the amount of land available for grazing.

Pigs seem to have been kept for domestic use, being useful only for meat and, once killed, were salted down for food over the winter. The inventory of Williams Bellis,[13] from Ty'n Llwyn in Llanfihangel Glyn Myfyr, who died in 1725, includes a 'flitch of bacon' worth 10s-0d. the number of pigs is not usually given, but two from Llanfihangel Glyn Myfyr do give more detail. Peter Morris,[14] from Cefn Post, who died in 1670, had '5 hoggs' worth £1-5s-0d and Robert John ap Hugh,[15] from Fotty had '2 swine' valued at £1-4s-0d. Poultry which would have included chickens, geese and ducks, were listed together with valuations from 1s-0d to 10s-0d. Presumably people would have been able to sell eggs that they did not need.

Over the summer months many animals, mainly cattle as well as poultry were taken by the drovers from all over north Wales, along well-trodden routes, to London to be sold in Smithfield Market. Many drovers started from Anglesey and came along the coast and down through the Vale of Clwyd. Others from this area followed a route which was later to become the A5 going along the Welsh border, through Birmingham and on to Essex. There the animals were left to graze for two or three weeks putting back some of the flesh lost on the journey, before being driven into London to be sold. Both cattle and poultry were shoed for this long journey, cattle with metal shoes and poultry were made to walk through wet tar which hardened on their feet. Aelwyd Brys, an old alehouse on the Cefn Brith road was a popular place for drovers to stop overnight leaving their animals safe in a nearby field. Others would have stopped in one of the two alehouses in the Llan and the blacksmith on the corner of the Denbigh road would have been busy mending and re-shoeing the cattle. Although we know that some people from Cerrigydrudion must have been drovers this was a part-time, summer occupation, no one is described as a 'drover' so it is not possible to identify anyone expect Edward Morris of Perthi Llwydion who was also a well known poet. The drovers were a respected group of men and, as well as driving cattle, sheep and poultry to London were entrusted by the community with a variety of jobs to do when they were there. These included taking valuables to sell and also buying goods nor available in north Wales. Before the development of banks some people asked them to collect money and deal with financial matters. Idris Evans[16] in his book about the drovers describes how they needed armed guards to protect them from highwaymen and opportunist thieves. When they returned with money for the stock sold as well as the goods they had purchased they also brought the latest news from London, new songs and ballads and information about friends and relatives they had met on the journey. Their role within the community was an important one for both farmers and for those needing help financially.

In 1660 the population of around 400 lived in farms along the valleys of Cwmpenanner and Cefn Brith, with a few people in Pentrellyncymer and around the Llan. All of these houses were built near springs or wells and, although many of the original buildings have either been altered or demolished, a lot of present day farms remain on the same site. The houses usually consisted of a main living room known as the kitchen, which would have had a peat fire for cooking and warmth, and close to the fire and oat chest. The loft room upstairs would have been reached by a ladder staircase and is where the children would have slept.

Houses varied in size depending on the money available and the needs of the inhabitants. All farms would have had a room outside, if possible on the north side where it would be cooler, to keep as a dairy or buttery. In 1729 John Davies,[18] of Llaethwryd's inventory listed 'all in the buttery 8s-0d'. They would also have had barns to store fodder and to keep cattle and horses in during the winter. It seems to have been quite common practice for families to build on to their house to accommodate children when they got married. People had to get permission to extend their properties or to build a new one from the local Justice of the Peace (an early form of Planning Permission). The custom of building a house in twenty four hours so that some was coming from the chimney known as Ty Nos must have taken place, but these were little more than wooden huts which have not survived, although permanent properties were probably built later on the site.

Houses were heated with peat fires. People would gather together with sledges and carts to gather the peat which was cut with special turbury knives,. Robert Richard's[19] inventory of 1736 lists 'turbury knives' worth 3s-0d which were used at Hafod y Maidd. The peat fire could be controlled to produce a slow heat useful for cooking stews and broths which were the mainstay of people's diets, but also be heated up to cook food in saucepans and frying pans.

Barley bread was eaten daily and baked in a container surrounded with peat as illustrated here.[21]

It is difficult to gain a detailed picture of people's diet because

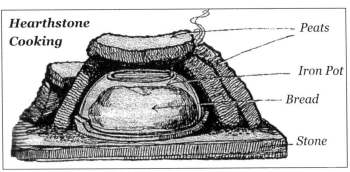

Peat Fire[17]

A variety of cooking pots.[20]

food is perishable and not mentioned in inventories or wills. However, we know that oats formed an important part of the daily diet, David Ellis,[22] of Garrwyd, Llanfihangel Glyn Myfyr's inventory of 1738, list an 'iron plate to bake oat bread' and we know these were very common.

Oats were kept in a warm place and used to thicken stews and broths as well as to make porridge with either milk or water. Flummery or llymru was a variation on porridge and oatcakes were broken up and mixed with warm or cold milk which helped

Oat chest with the distinctive sloping top.[23]

to fill people up. By 1720 there were three mills in the village, at Bwlch y Beudy, Pentrellyncymer and another at Hafod y Maidd. All these would have ground corn and produce the flour and crushed the oats needed in cooking, The Thomas Parry Charity supported two boys, Thomas, the son of Mathew John , who was apprenticed in 1716 to Robert Evan of Betws Gwerfyl Goch and in 1761 William Hughes to a local miller.

Although cows were kept mainly for their milk, sheep for their fleece and poultry for their eggs, these would have been killed when they got older and cooked in an iron pot with root vegetables such as turnips and parsnips to make a stew. Some meat including that from pigs would have been salted down to be used over the winter. No doubt people's diets were also supplemented by the occasional rabbit and fish from the river.

Most milk was turned into cheese and butter which was made in the kitchen or, in larger quantities, in the dairy. A lot of inventories list a cheesepress as well as cheese moulds and other containers.

Butter was also made and kept in butter tubs and firkins.

66

Some of the butter and cheese would have been sold locally and the rest taken to markets in Ruthin and Bala. Bread and cheese formed an important part of the diet and butter was used in cooking. Eggs could be boiled or fried, again inventories list frying pans and cooking pots. These were seen as very valuable and often passed on to children or other relatives in wills. Margaret Jones of Golden Gro, who died in 1769, left her niece 'a small round pan' which was to be passed to her daughter, Mary as well as an iron pot and frying pan to her sister.

Cheesepress [24]

These were made of iron or copper and as tea and coffee were introduced kettles began to be used to heat the water. These pans and kettles would have stood on a riddle over the fire so that they would not burn.

By the 1780s potatoes became very popular and were grown locally. The poor and others were encouraged to grown their own vegetables and some gardens were clearly quite large. The Baron Price Almshouses had a long piece of land at the back for gardens and Ty Tan y Mynwent (now the Parish Room) had a very large

Iron Cooking Pot

garden with sheds and outhouses (this is now the Lower Churchyard). As well as potatoes, turnips, parsnips, carrots, leeks and onion would have been grown and possibly cabbages and sprouts. It is very difficult to know if any fruit was grown. D. Hartley[25] in her comprehensive book on food mentions cloud berries'(Mwyar Berwyn) being made into tarts, blackberries, bilberries and blue berries as well as dandelion leaves being used in cheese sandwiches. Two old Welsh recipes are included, Welsh Rarebit (cheese on toast with ale) and 'punch neep', boiled potatoes and white parsnips mashed with butter. This may well have been eaten with boiled bacon. Bacon, cooked in a covered pot, was also eaten with pease pudding or dried beans. People probably used herbs, sometimes to disguise the taste of the meat, if it had been hung too long!

The majority of people would have had water and milk to drink as well as watered down ale. This was brewed locally in the alehouses

Trivet – to stand hot things on

and sold on, but some people had the equipment to brew their own ale. John Jones,[26] of Llanfihangel Glyn Myfyr, who died in 1729, had a brewing kitchen with three barrels and a firkin worth 15-0d. David Davies,[27] of Llaethwryd, who died in 1781 had one brewing pan valued at £3, six barrels and a firkin 13s-0d and two

68

mashing tubs and a cooler worth 12s-0d. He also had both a tea and coffee kettle. Tea and coffee were introduced to London by 1700 and various tea and coffee houses set up there and eventually in other large towns. David Davies was a wealthy man and may well have bought these back after a visit to London. Tea was sold to shops by licence and, as time went by, people would have been able to buy a variety of teas, firstly in market towns and then in villages across the country.

By 1760 there were one or two shops in the Llan but these began to grow as the population grew to over 1,000 and the demand for a wider variety of goods began to grow. People had relied on travelling salesmen, known as pedlars, who sold a wide variety of haberdashery material and some ironmongery, but as shops developed a wider variety of goods became available. It is interesting to note that Owen Thomas of Amlwch married a girl from the Llan in 1788 and set up a new shop and Robert Jones from Ruthin, who also married locally took over an existing shop, Ty'n Pwll, in 1791. By 1805 the white Lion had a shop and Cadwaladr Williams, tenant of Siop Ucha, next door to the White Lion ran a warehouse. The records of a shop in Penmorfa[28] on the north, west coast of Wales have survived for the period around the 1780's and 1790's. These show that the shop sold clothes and materials, nails, screws and medicine for 'ailing beasts'. Also soaps, starch, candles and 'blue' to whiten clothes, and a variety of food that kept for a comparatively long time such as tea, coffee, sugar, pepper, mustard cloves, ginger, raisins and currants. It is reasonable to assume that these goods would have been available in shops in Cerrigydrudion by the 1770's.

Abraham Dent[29] who ran a shop in Kirby Stephen in Lancashire during the same period also sold books including Bibles and various patent medicine such as Daffy's Elixir, *'a sure cure (under God) in most distempers, viz the Gout and Rheumatism, with all those torturing pains attending them, it takes away the Scurvy Root and Branch...is wonderful in the Stones and Gravel in the kidneys. 1s-3d'.* He sold apples and lemons and a lot of dried fruit as well as wine and spirits including rum, brandy and gin.

By the beginning of the nineteenth century far more travellers from England were beginning to visit Wales and alehouses began to offer wider services for visitors and entertainment. Both Aelwyd Brys and the White Lion seem to have had regular musicians with Richard Roberts in the White Lion and Robert David at Aelwyd Brys. One English traveller named Byng kept his bill from the Owen Glyndwr in Corwen in 1793. No doubt the alehouses around Cerrigydrudion would have offered something similar.

Dinners	2s - 6d
Supper	1s - 0d
Breakfast	10d
Tea & Coffee	9d
Wine	2s - 6d
Negus Brandy	1s - 0d
Punch Holands	1s - 0d
Cyder	
Ale & Beer	3d
Porter	
Tobacco	
Servants eating, ale,	
horses, hay, corn,	
chaise	4s-0d
	13s-4d

Although writing about a slightly later period Hugh Evans in Cwm Eithin (The Gors Glen) describes meals on local farms beginning with a breakfast of buttermilk, barley bread, cheese, oatcakes and butter with a dinner of broth, baked salt beef or yellow fat bacon, supplemented at harvest with rice pudding or plum dumpling. Tea at about four o clock would include 'siot' (shot) which was oatcakes baked hard and broken into warm or cold buttermilk or with brown bread crumbled into the buttermilk, followed by cheese. Sometimes tea would be 'bara canthreg', bread made with rye and wheat. Supper would usually be porridge. He points out that people also made bara brith and griddle cakes.

Over the hundred and fifty years there were a number of developments in farming which have continued up to the present day leading to better quality animals and meat, improved grass seeds and other crops and a wider variety of vegetables. With the growth of shops far more food stuffs were becoming available leading to improved nutrition and health. Life was very hard work for most people but there were opportunities to meet family and friends and to help each other when needed.

END NOTES
1   NLW. SA/1737/14.
2   NLW. SA/1685/94.
3   NLW. SA/1732/10.
4   NLW. SA/1736/12.
5   NLW. SA/1755/12.
6   NLW. SA/1685/
7   W. Davies.'The Agriculture of North Wales,' London. 1810. p.34.
8   NLW. SA/1732/10.
9   NLW. SA/1755/12.
10 Drawings from the Castle Museum, York.
11 NLW. SA/1726/18.
12 NLW. SA/1755/12.

13 NLW. SA/1725/52.

14 NLW. SA/1694/24.

15 NLW. SA/1723/98.

16 I. Evans. 'Hard Road to London.' Own publication. 2009. Available from Steptoe's Shop in Ruthin.

17 D.Hartley. 'Food in England.' London. 1955.

18 NLW. SA/1729/20.

19 NLW. SA/1736/12.

20 Drawings by Mrs. Biddy Greenwood, Glasfryn. 2000. With kind permission.

21 D. Hartlet. 'Food in England.' London. 1955.

22 NLW. SA/1729/143.

23 Drawing by Mrs. Biddy Greenwood, Glasfryn, 2000. With kind permission of The National Trust.

24 H. Evans. 'Cwm Eithin.' (The Gors Glen). Brython Press, Liverpool. 1936.

25 D.Hartley. 'Food in England.' London. 1955.

26 NLW. SA/1729./143.

27 NLW. SA/1758/151.

28 Hoh-Cheung and Lorna Mui. 'Shops and Shopkeeping in Eighteenth Century England.'London. 1986.

29 T.S.Willan. 'An Eighteenth Century Shopkeeper.' Manchester.. 1970.p.44.

Chapter 5

HOUSING, FURNISHING AND FASHION

The majority of people in the seventeenth and eighteenth centuries lived in small houses with one or two rooms downstairs and a loft above. Over time these houses developed names which usually described their location, such as Rhyd y Groes, a house by a ford at a crossroads, or their appearance, such as Tŷ Coch, the red house. Many of the houses and farms in the area today date back to the eighteenth century or even earlier and it is possible to locate nearly all the houses named in the church registers and other documents. Of course, these properties have been altered, extended and rebuilt over time, but many still show parts of their earlier origins.

Many families would have added an extension to their property to accommodate a newly married son and others would have built a separate house on their land. For example, by 1687 we find mention of a house in Cwmpenanner called Bron y Coed Derw and, by 1721 a second property called Votty Bron y Coed Derw, appears in the records. Many properties were called Votty, short for Hafoty, originally a summer dwelling house but, by 1700, lived in all the year round.

Houses were built of stone with wooden lintels above the doors and windows with the roof thatched with heathers or gorse mixed with clay, and attached to the wooden rafters. This would have needed replacing about every ten years and patched on a regular basis. Many houses were whitewashed inside and out to help seal the walls, with some properties using colouring outside. Besides Tŷ Coch, another house was called Bwlch y Maen Melyn, showing it was painted yellow, but most seem to have been white.

The majority of houses had floors made of compressed mud with rushes over them, but as the eighteenth century moved on, people began to lay either stone or slate slabs down making the house easier to keep clean. People seem to have heated their homes with peat fires and a number of inventories, such as that of Robert Richard,[1] of Hafod y Maidd, mention 'turbery knives' which were used for cutting peat. Windows were small and would have had glass in them, probably more like the leaded lights which are common in many churches, or wooden shutters which could be closed at night or if the weather was bad .

People had to have permission from the local Justice of the Peace before building a new house or extending an existing one, but this seems to have been a formality and there were certainly no complicated planning rules!

Most people seem to have moved into a house when they got married and stayed there all their married life. Owen William and Lowry moved into Pentre Cwm in 1737. By the time of Owen's death in 1783 his son Evan and daughter in law Ellin were living there. However, there were a few families who led very unsettled lives. Evan Jenkins and Anne Evan were married on 10 January 1769 and over the next twenty three years they had thirteen children and lived in at least eight different houses.

Houses and farms were built along the valley in Cwmpennaner where there were natural springs of water, and along the road that led through Cefn Brith with a few properties in Pentrellyncymer, again around water springs. The area around the Church, known as the Llan, where the church is situated, was on the crossroads with the road from Bala to Ruthin crossing the road from Corwen to Betws y Coed. This area saw a big growth in properties during the eighteenth century. By 1717 there were the two alehouses, Ty'n y Pwll, Ty Tan y Mynwent, the blacksmiths,

Tŷ Coch, the newly built Almshouse and a few small cottages including two owned by the church.[2] One was, by 1729, rented out to John Lawrence for £3 14s 0d per annum and is described as 'an alehouse with two fields'. By 1749[3] the church owned three houses, Robert Robert a 'victualler and blacksmith' lived in one, Robert William, a 'victualler' lived in the second and had a yard for turning horses and the Curate, Griffith Ellis lived in the third between 1746 – 1752. He and his wife Barbara had two children whilst living there.

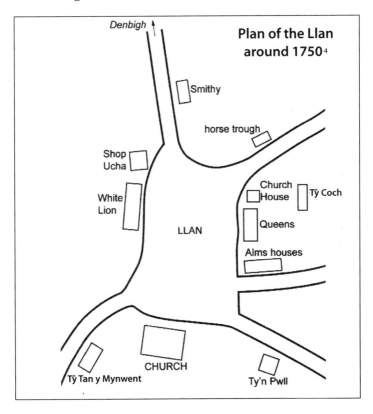

Plan of the Llan around 1750[4]

By the end of the eighteenth century there were a number of shops and more houses which spread out along the roads leading out of the village. Some of these were lived in by local tradesmen such as joiners, tailors, cobblers, masons and slaters.

In 1686 Edward Llwyd, an antiquarian,[5] sent out a questionnaire to all clergy asking for a whole variety of information including a list of 'the houses of note'. In Cwmpenanner these were Bwlch y Maen Melyn, Pentre Cwm, Llaethwryd and Tŷ

Mawr. On the front of Tŷ Mawr is the following inscription.[6]

By 1660 Evan Lloyd was living there and the house stayed in the same family for at least five generations with the fifth child of Evan Evans baptised in September 1812.

Clust y Blaidd around 1900.

76

In Cefn Brith he listed Hafod y Maidd, Clustyblaidd, (pictured here)[7] Glan Gors, Llechwedd Llyfn, Tai'n Foel, Ty'n y Graig and Ty'n Gilfach. He also included the houses Llyn y Cymmer and Bwlch y Beudy.

Also listed were 'properties of interest' these were, Aelwyd Brys, Perthi Llwydion, Pant y Griafolen, Nant y Ryryd [Irid], Nant y Krogwr, Kapelle and Llwyn Pilcot.

Houses were lit by the fire and with candles. Most people made their own candles by dipping reeds into melted tallow [animal fat] or wax. This would set and then burn down slowly. More wealthy people bought wax candles and a number of inventories mention candlesticks. By the turn of the century wax candles were on sale in local shops

The amount of furniture people had in their houses obviously depended on the size of the house and the amount of money they had. For most people the basic essentials would have been a wooden table and benches, a bedstead and bedding and chest to store clothes,[9] and another chest to keep oats which were a staple part of everyones' daily diet.

Drawing of a bed in Tŷ Mawr, Wybrnant, Penmachno.[8]

As time went by people would have acquired more furniture, another bed and bedding for the children, who would have slept upstairs in the loft which was reached  by a ladder staircase,[10] a wooden chair or two, perhaps with arms and more cooking pots, a cupboard to store food, a chest with drawers and maybe a dresser, would have been added over time.

All this furniture would have been made locally by carpenters and joiners who would have learnt their skills during an apprenticeship. Besides learning how to make basic furniture they would have also had to copy designs and decorations from other furniture and would, no doubt, have started to develop their own designs as time went by. Bedding and other material would have been spun or woven locally and quilts and pillows filled with feathers from ducks or geese.

The more well off had larger houses and much more furniture. The inventory of Gethin Lloyd of Clustyblaidd[11] made in 1726 includes three tables, including one round table as well as a long table and benches, seven chests, seven cupboards, two of these were 'press cupboards' and one 'a buttery cupboard, two desks, eight chairs in the parlour and two 'oak seats', five bedsteads and a lot of bed linen and 24 blankets, nine carpets, some of which may have been used to hang on the walls to keep out draughts and two jug and basin sets. There was also brass, silver and pewter vessels in the house. Everyone would have used pewter plates and tankards during this period, although china and pottery were becoming popular towards the end of the eighteenth century and many houses with a dresser began to display the blue and white china that is still very commonly seen on dressers today.

David Davies,[12] from Llaethwryd, who died in 1758 had by far the most furniture and possessions listed in any inventory from the area, although his is also the last inventory available for Cerrigydrudion. Besides the things listed in Gethin Lloyd's inventory for Clustyblaidd, he had a corner cupboard, a painted cupboard and a mirror, all very unusual outside of London in this period. Also, listed in the inventory were brewing equipment and tea and coffee making facilities as well as knives and forks. Forks

Drawing of a Cwpwrdd Tridarn in Tŷ Mawr, Wybrnant, Penmachno.[15]

were still a rarity in this area. A few people had a clock probably bought from one of the clockmakers in Denbigh or Wrexham. David Davies was a wealthy man and may well have purchased these luxury items on trips to London.

Many more inventories from Wales mention dressers, spinning wheels and screens, than comparable inventories for England and two dressers were left in wills. One by William Thomas of Capelle[13] in 1779 to his eldest daughter, Catherine, and the other by William Davies,[14] from Pen y Bryn to 'Margaret Owen, my old maid'.

The size of houses and their furnishings depended mainly on the income of the individuals concerned from tiny one roomed cottages to large eight to ten roomed houses. Furniture was valued and often passed on in wills. Beds and bedding were also often left to young relatives, to help them as they gathered their possessions together before they got married.

Another item that was sometimes left in wills was clothing. Most people would only have had a few clothes and it is noticeable that the clothing left is always described as 'my best clothing'. In 1694 Ales Burchinshaw,[16] of Llaethwryd left her sister, Sarah, 'her best mantle' and in 1707 Robert David,[17] from Elor Garreg left his 'best coat' to his cousin. Hugh Davies,[18] of Bryn Gwyn, who died in 1717, left his brother John, 'his best suit of clothing'. Mary David,[19] of Plas Onn who had been widowed after her daugher

A spinning wheel in Tŷ Mawr, Wybrnant, Penmachno.[20]

80

had grown up, had remarried. When she died in 1798 she left her daughter, Mary, 'her wedding apparal'.

Clothes would all have been made locally, either in the home, or by the tailors who lived in the community. With a large population of sheep, wool was easily available and was either used in material or for knitting. Spining wheels were quite common in homes and wills mention these being left to relatives Margaret Edwards,[21] from Pant y Mêl in Llanfihangel Glyn Myfyr left her granddaughter Margaret Wynne *'the larger spinning wheel which I direct my executors to deliver to her immediately after my decease.'*

There were also a number of weavers who would have woven cloth to be made into clothes and bed coverings. The Thomas Parry Charity funded quite a number of poor boys to be apprenticed as either tailors or weavers.

In the area were travelling salesmen known as pedlars, who moved around selling trimmings, buttons, lace, cottons and other similar goods. They would have attended the local fairs and village gatherings. With the growth of shops in the Llan, these items would have been available there as well.

Many people, both men and women, also earned extra money by knitting stockings, these were long socks that went over the knee. Skilled women could knit up to four pairs a week. In his book 'Cwm Eithin',[22] Hugh Evans described how *'Phebi knitted stockings to go over the knee and rode to Ruthin to sell them to the stocking man.'* Phebi was married to William David and in the early eighteen hundreds they lived in Tai Ucha, Cwm and then in Blaen Cwm.

For many jobs around the farm and other trades, gloves would have been useful and these seem to have been made of leather. Leather was also used to make shoes and when Cadwaladr ap

John,[23] of Llysan in Llanfihangel Glyn Myfyr in 1685 his invenyory listed 'leather, shoes, hemp and working tools' valued at £9 15s 0d and money he was owed amounting to £22 8s 2d.

The Overseers of the Poor gave money towards clothing and the residents of the Almshouses[24] were given new clohing annually. Clothes would have been kept in a wooden chest and as people began to own more clothes, larger chests with drawers in were made. The more wealthy obviously owned a wider selection of clothes and, if they travelled to large towns may well have been able to buy some 'ready made' clothes.

By the end of the eighteenth century ready made clothes were becoming available in shops throughout the country. In Robert's shop in Penmorfa on the north west coast of Wales they sold 'breeches, waistcoats, petticoats, hats and handkerchiefs'[25] It seems likely that these items and others, as well as material would have been available in the shops in Cerrigydrudion. Although there were fashions in clothes these would have taken a while to filter down to the countryside from the larger towns. Most people's clothes were made to be hard wearing and warm following basic patterns used for many years, although individuals probably added their own touches to them.

Between 1662-1812 we have seen a number of changes to the furnishings in houses to make them more comfortable and warmer. By 1812 a few houses had slate roofs, which, although expensive in the beginning, needed little maintenance and a growth in possessions especially china and cutlery.

END NOTES

[1]   NLW. SA/1736/12.
[2]   NLW. Rural Dean's Report for Rhos Deanery. 1729.
[3]   NLW. Rural Dean's Report for Rhos Deanery.
[4]   Computer generated by the Library, University of Aberystwyth.

5   DRO, The Parochialia.
6   Drawing by Mrs Biddy Greenwood, Glasfryn. 2000.
7   Photo kindly loaned by Miss G. Kynaston.
8   Drawing by Mrs. Biddy Greenwood, Glasfryn. 2000. With permission from The National Trust
9   Drawing by Mrs. Biddy Greenwood, Glasfryn. 2000. With permission from The National Trust.
10 Drawing by Mrs. Biddy Greenwood, Glasfryn. 2000. With permission from The National Trust.
11 NLW. SA/1726/18.
12 NLW. SA/1758/151.
13 NLW. SA/1779/16.
14 NLW. SA/1789/12.
15 Drawing by Mrs.Biddy Greenwood, Glasfryn. With permission from The National Trust.
16 NLW. SA/1694/23.
17 NLW. SA/11707//7.
18 NLW. SA/1717/5.
19 NLW. SA/1797/18.
20 Drawing by Mrs. Biddy Greenwood, Glasfryn. 2000. With permission from The National Trust.
21 NLW. SA/1794/71.
22 H. Evans. 'Cwm Eithin.' Brython Press, Liverpool. 1931. p.13.
23 NLW. SA/1685/94.
24 DRO. Records of the Baron Price Charity.
25 Hoi-Cheng and Lorna H. Mui. 'Shops and Shopkeeping in Early Modern England.' London. 1986. p219.

Chapter 6

LITERACY

For those of us living in the twenty-first century there is a great emphasis on the need to be able to read and write. Many jobs are only open to those who are literate and the western world's lifestyle is based on the written word and the ability to read it. With the advent of computers this has become even more important. Those unable to read and write are faced with limited work opportunities, the problems of dealing with any official business and the frustrations of not understanding much of what is happening in the world around them. This was not the case in the eighteenth century. There was a clear divide between being able to read and being able to white. A large proportion of the population had no need to write and if they had any official paperwork to do then they could easily ask the Parish Clerk or the Rector for help. Wealthier families would certainly have ensured that their sons could read and write and had a good education at a local grammar school such as Ruthin, Llanrwst or Wrexham before attending University in Oxford or Cambridge. The daughters of wealthier families would also have learnt to read and write and had some education from their mother or a governess.

However, by the middle of the eighteen century the numbers of people who could read had grown considerably and there was a lot of encouragement to read the Bible and other Christian books. The Rural Dean[1] reported that in 1729 there were 'two little reading schools' in Cerrigydrudion and eighty years later the churchwardens[2] reported that the Methodists keep a school in the meeting house for about twenty young children who are taught to write and read the Bible. This was part of a rapidly growing movement throughout Wales to promote reading and most communities would have ad some sort of 'reading school'. This was aimed mainly at enabling people to read the Bible, but made it possible for them to read other books as well.

Before 1695 books could only be printed in London. This meant that books written in Welsh were put together by non-Welsh speakers leading to any number of mistakes. We need to remember that the spelling of Welsh was not standardised during this period although a dictionary was published in 1688 attempting to do this.

Thomas Jones, from Corwen, did set up a printing press in London but moved to Shrewsbury after 1695 along with John Rhydderch. They began printing books in Welsh which were distributed all over North Wales with about 545 titles were produced between 1660 – 1730. The Bible was the most important book to be published and from 1700 onwards The Society for the Propogation of Christian Knowledge (SPCK) began to subsidise the printing of Bibles, Prayer Books and other Christian books making them accessible to nearly everyone. Between 1660 – 1730 over 40,000 copies of the Bible were produced in Welsh with many given away free to 'the deserving poor'. These were Bibles intended for people to read at home and cost 4s – 5s-6d depending on the binding. A larger print Bible was produced in 1690 for use in Churches. By 1770 Peter Williams was producing the Bible in serial form charging 1s for each part. The 1662 Prayer Book was translated into Welsh by 1664 and regularly reprinted. Parishes could buy these for 18s- a dozen. All these books were transported by carrier from London or Shrewsbury to Chester, and then by more local carrier to towns such as Llanrwst, Wrexham, Bangor and Denbigh. In 1749 Robert

Containing many more British words than are in Dr. Davies's *Antiquæ Linguæ Britannicæ Dictionarium duplex.*

FIRST,
Explaining the hard British words, by more familiar work in the same Tongue: very useful for all such as desire to understand what they Read in that Language.

SECONDLY,
Shewing the Proper English to every British word:
And consequently,
The true way of Spelling all words in both Languages.

Amplified
With the Geographical names of Countreys, Counties, Cities, Towns and places in Great Britain (and some beyond Sea) in the Ancient British, and present English.

Whereunto are added
Plain and easie Directions to Welshmen for the true pronouncing of the English Tongue by a short Introduction in the British Language.

With the proper use or signification of all accents, points or stops, as now used in the British and English: being necessary to be understood by every Reader.

Compiled by the great Pains and Industry of THO. JONES.

Printed 1688. and Sold in *London* by Mr. *Lawrence Baskervile* at the Red Lion in *Aldermanbury*, and Mr. *John Marsh* at the Red Lion in *Cateaton-ftreet.*

Yn Cynwys llawer mwy o eiriau Cymraeg, nag fydd yng Eirlyfr y Difgawdr Siôn Defi o Gymraeg a Lading.

Yn gyntaf,
Yn hyfpyfu meddwl y Gymraeg deheitht, drwy gymraeg amwy Cynacfmol : yr hyn fy gyfaen, a dcauyddiol iawn i bawb a Ewyllyfient ddeall a ddarfllenant yn gymraeg.

Yn Ail,
Yn dangos y gwir Saefnaeg i bôb gair Cymraeg.
Ag yn dilynyol,
Y môdd i gyfllhu, fef i (ffpelio) pôb gair yn gwir yn y gumraeg, a'r Saefnaeg.

Ac a helaethwyd
Ag Arrgraphyddol henwau Gwledydd, Gofgordion, Dinasoedd, Trefydd, a mannau (ymmpyrddun fawr, a Rhai dros y meir:) yn yr hêu gymraeg, a'r bresennol Saefnaeg.

At yr hyn a chwanegwyd
Eglur, a hylaw Athrawiaeth, (i'r Cymry) am gywir Adroddiad y Saefnaeg; drwy fyr Byfordddiad yn yr faith gumraeg.

Gyda phriodor ddeunydd neu Arwyddoccad yr hôll orddignau, a'r Atnalion, fy'r Anvuu yn Arferedig yn y gymraeg a'r Saefnaeg; Ag yn Angenrheidiol eu deall gan bôb darllennydd.

A gafgluwyd drwy ddirfawr boen, a diwydrwydd Tho Jones.

Argraffwyd 1688. ac ar werth yng Bhecrhydd gan Mr-Lawrence Bafkervrie Tân Luu y llew Coch yn yr hendaber-Rceni, a chan Mr. John Marth tan Lûn y Llew Côch yn rhewl Câth-ftwbftâd.

The front of the first Dictionary published in Welsh and English by Thomas Jones in 1688. [3]

Jones, the Rector of Llanycil, wrote to the Bishop of St. Asaph on 8 May 1749,[4] *'I perceived that Mr. Watts was about sending the Welsh Bibles which are at Chester and which I shall receive by the Bala carrier at the latter end of this week and I shall dispose of them as fast and with discresion as I can.'*

There was also a growing market for books about Christianity by clergy and lay people. Edward Samuel, who was Rector of Betws Gwerfyl Goch from 1702 – 1720, translated a number of books into Welsh, which were published by John Rhydderch. These included:

1713 Prif Ddylestswydd Gristion (The Chief Duties of a Christian)
1716 Holl Ddylestswydd Dyn (The Whole Duty of Man)
1723 Gwirionedd y Grefydd Gristnogawl (The Truths of ye faith)
1731 Athrawiaeth yr Eglwys Cristnogol (The Teachings of the Christian Church)

Bishop Beveridge of St. Asaph established a library for clergy and wrote a Welsh teaching book to help clergy teach those preparing for Confirmation.

Some wills mention that people left Bibles and Prayer Books. For example, John Jones,[5] of Pant y Mêl, Llanfihangel Glyn Myfyr left 'a large Bible' valued at 18s in 1729. Margaret Jones,[6] of Golden Gro who died in 1769 left her Prayer Book to her brother, William, and, in 1798 William Thomas,[7] of Ty Mawr left a 'large Bible' to his sister, Elizabeth.

In 1621 Edmund Prys translated the Psalms into popular Welsh meters to be sung in church and to help people memorise the Psalms. This book was usually published with the Bible or Prayer Book. By the end of the seventeenth century people were writing Welsh hymns and carols and these carols became very popular especially at the Christmas Plygain Services. Early on Christmas morning people walked to Church, often carrying special Plygain candles, and singing the newly written carols. Then they gathered in Church to sing further carols with smaller groups performing items. The Churchwardens accounts for Betws Gwerfyl Goch list the purchase of these special Plygain candles by 1720 indicating that they were holding a Plygain and in 1745 a large collection of Plygain Carols and hymns was published called 'Carolau a Dyriau Duwiol'.[8] Many of these carols are still sung today. It needs to be stressed that welsh was the language in general use. In 1749 the Rural Dean wrote about Llanfihangel Glyn Myfyr, *'It needs to be noted that services were all taken in Welsh as there is scarce a word of English understood in this part of the country and therefore no need of English prayers or sermon.'* [9]

Besides Christian books there was an enormous growth in the publication of annual almanacs, printed ballads, small story books and books on specific subjects such as *'The Compleat Parish Officer,'*which listed the different jobs within the community, such as the Constable, and detailed their roles.

Printers also began to produce a selection of primers, which were books designed to help both adults and children to read. These would have been on sale in local shops, including Cerrigydrudion, ranging in price from 1d – 6d. This enabled even quite poor people to buy them. A number of inventories list books including Robert Jones of Hafod y Llan, who died in 1723 leaving books worth £2, John Cadwaladr from Elor Garreg whose books were valued at 15s in 1729 and David Davies who died in 1758 left £2 3s 0d worth of books at Llaethwryd.

During this period the Church and community were entirely Welsh speaking. All services were conducted in Welsh and people's everyday language was Welsh. The only people with a good knowledge of English would have been those who had attended a grammar school where they would also have learnt Latin, so that they could read classical literature. A University education was based large around knowledge of Greek and Latin and was taught entirely in English. In a community like Cerrigydrudion the Rector, the Parish Clerk and a few other wealthy gentry families, would have had this extensive knowledge of Welsh, English and Latin. Until 1735 the Church registers had to be filled in using Latin. This was very basic and Latin does not seem to have been used for anything else. All other legal documents, such as wills, inventories, bonds and records from the Denbishshire Session Rolls were in English and printed documents including those used by the overseers of the Poor were also printed in English. It is interesting to note that the Churchwardens' Accounts for Llanuwchllyn, which list the day to day expenditure of the Church are in Welsh, and written by a variety of people, but the official, annual report is written in English.

Because there is little remaining written material in Welsh it is difficult to know how many people could write in Welsh, presumably far more than could write in English. A number of wills were written by the local Rector and Parish Clerk. They would have translated the person's wishes into English before asking them to sign or make a mark witnessed by two others. Some tradesmen and people running businesses, such as an alehouse or shop must have had some ability to keep records in a written form, and a number of inventories list money owing to the deceased. The Inventory of a shoemaker, Cadwaladr John,[10] from Llysan, Llanfihangel Glyn Myfyr, who died in 1685 lists a total of £27 8s 2d in outstanding bills including £9 from Robert

Roberts! 7s.0d from Roger Griffiths and 3s 2d from Thomas Parry.

It has been assumed that by looking at whether people signed, put their initials or just a cross, when they got married or made a will, one could see how many people could write. A study of the marriage registers for Cerrigydrudion shows that quite a number of people, who put their initials or a cross could write in later life. Again, people who did not sign their name on wills could certainly write when they were younger, for example, David Maurice of Llaethwryd wrote, in a very legible hand, the will of Margaret Thomas who died in 1711, but had someone else to write his own will in 1729, and signed with a very shaky hand. Perhaps he had had a stroke or some other illness. Other people who one would have expected to sign their wills just managed their initials. These include John Hughes, a wealthy pedlar from the Llan, with land in Corwen, who died in 1709, John Lawrence, an educated man from Glan Gors, who died in 1750 and Charles Row lands, who was the innkeeper at Ceirnoge, until his death in 1802.

It is also interesting to note that even wills and inventories written in English use a number of Welsh words. Cyst (chest) appears frequently in lists of furniture and hobbit or hobbaid, meaning a stone in weight, is often used. Owen ap Robert,[11] of Hafod y Llan's inventory made in 1748, list '24 hobbits of oatmeal'.

We also need to remember that many people wrote poetry using the special Welsh metre patterns. The most famous poet from this area was Edward Morris, who was born in Perthi Llwydion in July 1733, the eldest son of Maurice ap Hugh and Lowry vch Edward. He may have attended grammar school in Ruthin or Llanrwst and at some point became attached to two wealthy households, where he developed and used his poetic skills. These were the households of Sir Thomas Mostyn at Gloddaeth (now St David's College near Llandudno) and Bodysgallen, the home of Robert Wynne. Edward Morris worked as a drover, a seasonal occupation, taking large flocks of sheep, cattle and geese from north Wales to sell in the area around London. During the winter months he seems to have spent time with his two patrons at Gloddaeth and Bodysgallen.

By 1661 he had married Sarah Davies, with whom he had six children.

Edward Morris and Sarah Davies

David	Alice	Maurice	Son	John	Margaret
1662	1670	1672	1674	1676	1678
			(died)		

Edward Morris wrote a wide variety of poems which have been collected together by Gwenllian Jones for her MA in 1941, but sadly have never been published. He died, while working as a drover, in Braintree in Essex in 1689, and was buried there.

There were clearly other poets whose work has not survived, as well as some poetry written by unknown poets including the eulogy on the memorial to Baron Price's mother, Margaret, who died in 1723. This large Memorial is in the Geeler Chapel in Cerrigydrudion Church[12] and reads as follows:-

> Marget Prys ddilys a ddaeth on Enwog
> Ac union waeddiaeth
> Cadd hîr ffeiniol Fywolaeth
> Gras a dawn, ac at Crist aeth.

Mae Fustus Cafas cyflawn gwiw lasol
Ac Eglwyswyr doethion
Barwniaid Barnwyr union
Hynod yn hanfod a bon.

Bendithion llawniar fel llû a gafodd
Drwy Gyfan Haelioni
Boed canmil oi heppil hi
Addas a thebys ynddi.

(Sincere Margaret Price became famous
And uprightly endowed
She enjoyed a long and fine life
Grace and talent, and she went to Christ.

Upright and remembered fine Magistrate
And wise churchmen
And Baron Judges
Notable descended from her.

She enjoyed many full blessings
Through complete generosity
Let there be one hundred thousand of her progeny
Worthy, and of her nature.)

There were also the lighter, songs and ballads that became very popular during the eighteenth century. These include the writings of Jack Glan Gors who was born in 1767,

Jac Glan Gors. [13]

Jac was the eldest of the three children of Lawrence John and Margaret Roberts. Lawrence was 51 when he married Margaret aged 23 on 29 January 1766. He played an active role in the community serving twice a Churchwarden. He died aged 75, in December 1790. Jac Glan Gors, along with his cousin Edward Jones seem to have been causing some problems in the community at the end of the 1780's and the local law enforcers decided to call in the militia to have the two young men with others enlisted in the army. Jac avoided this enlistment and moved to London where he was influenced by the writings and dogma of Thomas Paine. Paine had been influenced by the French Revolution and was keen to see the overthrow of the royal family, the power of the government overturned and the church destroyed. Jac wrote two revolutionary tracts 'Seren Tan Gwmwl' in 1795 and 'Torraid y Dydd' in 1797 which followed this theme.

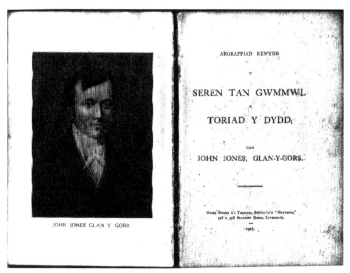

Picture of the front of the copy of the book
containing both tracts. [14]

For a while Jac moved back to north Wales when the situation became difficult in London but by 1800 he was back in London running the Kings Head in Ludgate Hill. He was one of the founder members of the 'Cymdeithas y Cymreigyddion' and a strong supporter of the newly formed 'British and Foreign Bible Society' along with Thomas Charles of Bala. His poems and ballads include 'Dic Sion Dafydd,' 'Sessiwn yng Nghymru' and 'Offeiriad yn Sir Aberteifi,' and were set to well-known tunes of the period. On 23 July 1816 Jac, aged 49, married Jane Mondell Whitehouse. He died aged 54 on 21 May 1821 and was buried in St George's Church near St Paul's Cathedral. In 2003 E.G. Millward published a collection of Jac's poetry entitled 'Cerddi Jac Glan y Gors.'

Priodas Siencyn Morgan

Sef Cân Newydd yn gosod allan ddull priodasau yng Nghymru

Tôn: Drops of Brandy

Mae llawer o droeau'n y byd
   Yn haeddu cael eu cofio,
Er hynny, o bryd i bryd,
   Mae'r cwbl yn mynd yn ango';
Os nad yw yn drosedd mawr
   Yn erbyn y dull sy rŵan,
Wel, be' fyddai cofio'n awr
   Am briodas Siencyn Morgan?

'Roedd Siencyn am chwarae pêl
   Yn fawr ei glod trwy Gymru,
A gwasgu, doed a ddêl,
   Y merched ar y gwely;
Am fedi a lladd gwair
   'Roedd Siencyn yn eitha' gweithiwr,

One of the ballads written by Jac Glan Gors. [15]

During the eighteenth century there was an enormous rise in peoples' ability to read which was reflected in the thousands of books which were published in Welsh. This enabled many people to read the Bible for themselves, as well as follow services in Church with a Prayer Book and join in with hymn singing. There must have been many informal get-togethers in homes and alehouses for people to sing the ballads and hymns that they heard. Although we know that many people could write, as well as read, but because far less emphasis was placed on writing, there is much less evidence.

END NOTES

1   NLW. Rural Dean's Report for Rhos Deanery. 1729.
2   NLW. Churchwardens' Report for Cerrigydrudion. 1809.
3   Available in NLW.
4   NLW. Letter in the papers of the Diocese of St. Asaph.
5   NLW. SA/1729/143.
6   NLW. SA/1769/7.
7   NLW. SA/1798/120.
8   Available from the NLW.
9   NLW. Rural Dean's Report for Rhos Deanery. 1749.
10 NLW. SA/1695/94.
11 NLW. SA/1748/
12 Photo of the memorial taken by Myrddin ap Dafydd. Translation by Dr. E.E.J.Davies, Cerrigydrudion.
13 This is a copy of the picture which is hanging in the Coffee Bar at Cerrigydrudion School.
14 Kindly loaned by Mr. J.F.Williams, Cerrigydrudion.
15 Taken from E.W.Millward 'Cerddi Jac Glan y Gors' Llandybie. Gwasg Dinefor. 2003.

Chapter 7

CRIME AND PUNISHMENT

As in every century, the eighteenth had its share of crime. The local Parish Vestry elected a Constable each year whose role was to check on local and mostly petty crime. According to the *'Compleat Parish Officer'*[1] there were seventy six areas where he could intervene, which included checking that millers were giving the correct weight of flour, fining people up to 5s for drunkeness, locating the father's of illigitimate children so that they could pay maintenance and closing down unlicensed alehouses. This work had to be done on a voluntary basis and, as the century moved on, it became an increaslingly unpopular job as it took up a great deal of time and left the person open to threats and assaults. If crimes were seen to be serious by the Constable then they would be passed on to the local Justice of the Peace.

These people were appointed by the county officials and dealt with cases that went to the Quarter Sessions for trial in Ruthin. Quite often clergy served as Justices and three Rectors of Cerrigydrudion, namely Evan Wynne, Humphrey Humphries and James Price, were among that number. In 1655 the Justices set up a House of Correction in Ruthin. The Justices kept a record of all the cases and these were collected together at the end of each year and bound together and are stored in the Denbighshire Record Office in Ruthin.[2] They have now been listed and are available to the general public.

In the four parishes of Cerrigydrudion, Llanfihangel Glyn Myfyr, Llangwm and Ysbyty Ifan, the most common crime was assault, often when people had been drinking. Other cases included incitment to riot, theft, trespass, hunting with

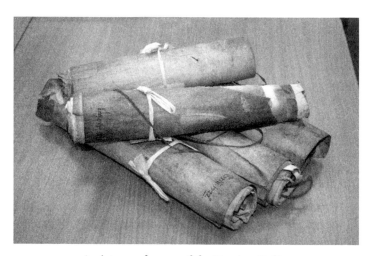

A picture of some of the Session Rolls.[2]

greyhounds on Christmas Day and rape. A number of people, both men and women, were bound over to keep the peace.

On 28 April 1768 Lewis Lloyd,[3] a Victualler, was called as a witness by Humphrey Humphries to give evidence against Evan Evans of Ty Rhedyn, Llanfihangel Glyn Myfyr and Cadwaladr Thomas of Blaen Eiddon, Ystbyty Ifan, for *'assaulting Morgan Pugh of Llanddew, Aberarth in Cardiganshire.'* This incident shows that people travelled large distances but also the probable suspicion of locals had for strangers.

Those bound over to keep the peace included Ann,[4] wife of John Hughes, a wealthy pedlar, who lived in the Llan. Her husband and John Robert of Llandorren, Merioneth, her son-in-law, each paid £20 as a Bond so that she would keep the peace.

Only landowners were allowed to use greyounds to hunt for game and the problem seems to have been that Robert Lloyd,[5] of

Hafod y Maidd was doing so on a Sunday and Hugh Hughes from Tyn y Waen on Christmas Day, both being days when it was illegal to hunt for game.

The Great Sessions dealt with more serious cases and the records for these are available in the National Library of Wales in Aberystwyth. Between 1733 – 1811, in Cerrigydrudion, there were three cases of riot and assault, two thefts, two cases of infanticide and one of forgery. In Llangwm there were four cases of theft, three of riot and assault, one murder and one case of avoiding conscription to the military. In Llanfihangel Glyn Myfyr there were two cases of riot and assault, one of breaking and entering and a case of arson. On the whole people were declared to be not guilty.

Aelwyd Brys was a busy alehouse on the Cefn Brith road, with travellers staying overnight on their way to Llanrwst and through the mountains to the coast, or south east to Corwen and Llangollen. On 15 April 1715 William Rowland,[6] of Aelwyd Brys, a yeoman, accused Griffith Evans of the theft of, '*1 blanket, 1 sheet, 3 petticoats,1 shirt, 1 flannel shift, 1 mantel, 1 hatt, 1 flannel waistcoat, 1 yards of white flannel, 1 yards of coloured cloth and 1 bolster.*' Presumably these were clothing and bedding from the alehouse. David Jenkin of Havod Escob, Llanfor, was called to give evidence . There is no record of the outcome.

In Cerrigydrudion it is noticeable that those involved with cases of riot and assault were usually yeomen or gentlemen. In 1749 David Williams,[7] a bachelor from Rhyd y Cae, along with Thomas Jones, a yeoman of Bron Llaethwryd, David Davies, a wealthy gentleman living at Llaethwryd and Edward Edwards, a yeoman, ' broke down the hedges and fences of an enclosed piece of land called the Ffrith', owned by Edward Jones, a gentleman, of Ty Mawr'.

Then in 1779,[8] William Jones, Evan Evans and David Evans 'broke down the hedge and fences around the house of Robert Jones, who was so seriously injured 'his life was despaired of.'

In December 1792 [9] sheep belonging to the Rector, Revd. James Price, were stolen from the pound by John William and David Jones. The eleven ewes, eleven weather sheep and eleven others were found grazing in a field of turnips near Bryn Saint on land adjoining the Rectory.

A Law passed in 1624 stated that a mother needed a witness to state that her child had been born dead, otherwise it would be assumed that the dead child had been murdered by its mother. The woman would have to face examinations by local Midwives, the Overseers of the Poor and the Constable. This law would have especially affected women expecting an illegitimate child, as they may well have been trying to hide the pregnancy. In 1768 Jane Williams, a servant, who had moved into the area, was working at the Mill in Hafod y Maidd when she was accused of murdering her new born child. A yeoman, John Williams,[10] from Ty Tan y Graig, put a Bond of £10 with the local Justice Humphrey Humphries and witnesses were called. One Elizabeth, was a relative of John William and the others, all women, who lived near Hafod y Maidd were, Catherine Roberts, a widow from Hafod y Maidd, a spinster, Alice Evans of Hafotty Hafod y Maidd, Mary, wife of Robert Hughes of Cefn Hir Fynydd and Jane Roberts of Pant y Griafolen. Jane Williams was sent to gaol in Ruthin but eventually declared not guilty.

In 1803 the law was changed so that the prosecutors had to prove the child had been born alive and subsequently been murdered. In 1811,[11] Magdalen Evans, also an unmarried servant, was accused of murdering her baby. A vivid account of the case was recorded as follows:

being big with male child, did bring forth the said child, and in secret, which said male child so being born alive was a bastard and that ye said Magdalen Evans not having the fear of God before her eyes, but being moved and instigated by the Devil on the fourteenth day of March, as soon as the male child was born, with force of arms, being feloniously and wilfully of her malice aforethought, did make an assault with both hands in the mouth of the said child fixed and placed in the mouth, face and cheeks of the sad child, and did tear, render and lacerate, giving unto the said child several mortal wounds in and upon the mouth, face, cheeks and palate, and of which several mortal wounds the child instantly died.'

Three women were called as witnesses and a surgeon Robert Nicholls examined her and she was declared to be innocent. No records exist which show what happened to her after this traumatic event.

The final case recorded from Cerrigydrudion concerns forgery. By the end of the eighteenth century various individuals were beginning to set up banks and issue money. It is noticeable that most wills state that any money left in wills was to be in 'lawful British money'. With the growth of banks came a growth in the forging of banknotes. Drovers, who were trusted to carry large amounts of money to London and back for local people, were some of the victims caught up in the growth of forged notes. In 1805 [12] three men were accused of having forged £1 notes, William Morris, a drover from Llangwm and Cerrigydrudion and William Ffoulkes from Betws Gwerfyl Goch were not prosecuted, but John Roberts was found to be guilty and sentenced to be transported for fourteen years. The records note that William Ffoulkes told the court that *'he could get as many notes as he liked at a place between Wolverhampton and Birmingham, a hamlet, where the men lately executed in Ruthin were apprehended.'*

There are a number of other cases on the Quarter Session Rolls for Denbighshire which were seen to be criminal offences then but would not fall into that category today. The first of these was a failure to maintain the roads. All householders had to give four days labour and those with land worth more than £50 had to provide a cart and animals to pull it as well as two able men. Most roads were little more than 'green lanes' which were suitable for the movement of people on foot, horses, pack horses and mules and for herds of animals to move around, but as people began to use carts and carriages the roads needed to be better looked after. The Turnpike Trusts,[13] established at the end of the eighteenth century, charged people to travel along the roads and then used that money to upgrade the roads. The costs were:

Coaches 4d

Wagon, carts and sledges 3d

Horses, laden or unladen 1d

Droves of cattle 10d for every 20

Droves of calves, hogs, sheep and goats 5d for every 20

In 1798 Jane Roberts of Pant y Griafolen,[14] was summoned *'for not taking a team of horses to perform three days duties.'* Her son Edward Edwards paid the fine of £1 – 10s. The records for Llanfihangel Glyn Myfyr show two cases where the roads were destroyed by 'extraordinary flooding' one at Llysan in 1744,[15] and the other in 1793,[16] where floods further along the river Alwen caused so much damage to the bridge that it needed to be rebuilt.

Some cases referred to the Law of Settlement. This meant that everyone had to have a parish where they resided. Women who married someone from another parish became the responsibility of that parish should their husband die, leaving them with no visible means of support. The Overseers of the Poor were responsible for paying maintenance for those who were in need but were very diligent in sending people back to another parish if they could do so. A printed form was filled in and sent to the Overseers of the relevant parish who would try to see if there were any loopholes they could use to avoid accepting these people. If they could not then a form was sent back and the people removed. As the century moved on the money available to provide for the poor had to be stretched further as the population grew and the number of removals increased. The following account shows what was involved in organising the removal of Jane William, a widow, from Nantglyn to Cerrigydrudion in 1775.[17]

The Rectory, Cerrigydrudion

	£	s	d
Attended overseers to take instruction		6	0
Drawing notice of appeal, copy and service		10	0
Payment to file order for Appeal		3	6
Payment for order or Adjournent		2	0
Motion consenting to Adjournment		3	6
Quarters Session fee	1	1	0
Easter 1775			
Quarter Session fee to Mr Lloyd	1	1	0
Same fee to Mr William	1	1	0
Attending to examine witness, drawing brief		6	0
Brief for Mr Lloyd		3	4
To Clerk in Chambers for reading file and quashing order for removal		9	0
Notice to tax costs and copy		4	0
My Clerk's journey to serve respondents at Nantglyn and his attendance to prove such Notice on taxing costs	1	4	0
To the pauper for her maintenance from the time of removal to the quashing of the order	1	12	6
Robert John Rowland, witness, for his attendance at the Quarter Session in Ruthin to be examined by Mr William, being out three days, horse hire and expenses		12	0
The like, to Catherine Owen another witness		12	0
Drawing bill and copy		4	0
Payent to clerk of the Peace, taxing the same		6	0
Attending taxation		4	0
Copy order and bill of costs to be served on the Nantglyn overseers		4	0
Service thereof		5	0
	10	4	4
Allowed John Hughes Deduct	4	12	8
	5	**11**	**8**

This shows the legal work involved and the care taken to ensure that Jane William, a widow in need, was properly looked after.

Two other cases also show how the Settlement Act worked. On 5 April 1764 a removal order was issued by the Overseers of the Poor for William Robert, his wife, Jane, and their two children, Catherine aged two, and Jonett just two weeks old, to be removed to Llannefydd parish. The couple had been married in 1761 and must have fallen on hard times. They lived in the Llan in Cerrigydrudion and it appears that the Overseers in Llannefydd refused this application. In 1773 they were still living in the Llan when William Robert died. The second case concerns the family of William Evans. He was from Llanfiangel Glyn Myfyr, but, having married Catherine on 12 May 1783, they settled in the Llan in Cerrigydrudion, where they had three children, Sarah aged seven, Catherine aged 5 and Gwen, a year old. On 22 March 1794 Williams Evans was buried and his wife and children left destitute. Because William came from Llanfihangel the Overseers of the Poor in Cerrigydrudion issued a removal order for the family on 4 June 1794 and they had to move to Llanfihangel.

The Session Rolls also list some cases of vagrancy. Vagrants were people who could not establish a parish of settlement and roamed the countryside hoping to find work and a roof over their heads. Some were women who were expecting an illegitimate child, others were probably people with some sort of mental illness and some may have committed a crime and be running away from the Law. The church records mention the burial of vagrants, often found under a hedge or in a barn. One case highlights the difficulties faced by people when the Settlement Act was enforced. On 20 December 1771 Humphrey Humphries issued a vagrancy pass for Elizabeth Davies,[19] and her three children who were travelling to Cardigan, the last settlement of her late husband Thomas Davies, who had been a Sergeant in Colonel Webb's regiment. The pass required the Overseers of the

Poor in the communities they passed through, to provide for the family on their journey.

The next group of cases found in the Session Rolls concerned the issuing of summonds for the fathers of illegitimate children to be declared so that they could pay maintenance for these children. If the father was not named then the overseers of the Poor were liable for the costs of raising the child. They were very few illegitimate children with the number only rising at the end of the century when there was already a lot of pressure on the finances of the Overseers.

Lastly, the Session Rolls contain a number of 'Sacrament Certificates'. These were copies of a form issued by the Rector and Churchwardens to state that the person had made their communion at Easter. On 13 July 1718 [20] a certificate was issued for William Price Esquire of Cernioge, and another issued on 14 May 1727 [21] for Cadwaladr Wynne of Foelas. Both stated that they had attended Church in Ysbyty Ifan. During the eighteenth century many jobs and university colleges were only open to members of the Church and these certificates were used to prove the person's allegiance.

No doubt quite a lot of criminal activity went unrecorded. If discovered it might well have been dealt with informally with only persistent offenders being taken to court. It would appear that drunkeness was one of the main causes of the fighting and assaults which took place. For details of Edward Jones who committed a whole series of crimes in 1795, see the chapter on 'Meet the People'.

END NOTES
[1] *The Compleat Parish Officer*. First pub 1743 facsmilie copy made by the Wiltshire Historical Society
[2] DRO. CD ROM Denbighshire Session Rolls
[3] DRO. QSD/SR/270/3
[4] DRO. QSD/SR/7/28
[5] DRO. QSD/SR/361/51-52

6   NLW. GSR/4/50/2
7   NLW. GSR/4/59/3
8   NLW. GSR/4/63/5
9   NLW. GSR/41/56/33
10 NLW. GSR/4/69/3
11 NLW. GSR/7/67/6
12 RT Prichard. '*Denbighshire Roads and Turnpike Trusts*' Transactions of the Denbighshire Historical Society No 12. p 89
13 DRO. QSD/SR/351/33
14 DRO. QSD/SR/143/23
15 DRO. QSD/SR/335/30
16 DRO. QSD/SR/337/57 & 58
17 DRO. QSD/SR/220/48-49
18 DRO. QSD/SR/337/36 and 339/25
19 DRO. QSD/SR/248/6-7
20 DRO. QSD/SR/40/25
21 DRO. QSD/SR/74/1

Chapter 8

THE ROLE OF THE CLERGY

When a new Rector was appointed to a parish it would be clear to his parishioners exactly what his duties were. Firstly, to conduct Sunday Services, preach and celebrate a monthly Communion Service and to take a service on Saint's Days. Secondly, to baptise, take weddings and funerals and, after the Morning Service, to conduct a short service of thanksgiving for the birth of a child, known as Churching. Thirdly, to visit the sick and the dying and to care for the needy. In Cerrigydrudion there were a number of Charities set up to provide for the poor and the Rector was one of the administrators of these. His other duties were wide-ranging including paper work for the Diocese and individuals within the parish, preparing young people for Confirmation, possibly serving as a Justice of the Peace and organising and collecting tithes and other financial dues (A list of the Rectors in Cerrigydrudion can be found at the end of this chapter).

The Rector was expected to live in the Rectory which until around 1790 in Cerrigydrudion was a small, two-storied house with a parlour, kitchen, buttery and study on the ground floor and bedrooms upstairs, as well as a number of outbuildings and land. The house would have been similar to many farmhouses in the area and it was the Rector's responsibility to maintain it. This seems to have worked fairly well in Cerrigydrudion but presented a number of problems in other parishes including Betws Gwerfyl Goch where, in 1729[1] *'the house had a good number of rooms but only an indifferent appearance, with the thatching in a poor state. The windows were low, small and filthy and the floors all earthern. It stood in a very exposed position and was very damp'*. The Rector, Mr Edward Jones, *'did not reside at Betws, but lived in Llanfawr, six, hearty, Welsh miles away. He, for his own part, was quite prepared to live in the parsonage house provided, but he could not prevail on his wife to move to Betws,'* Towards the end of the century there was a dispute between the new Rector and the former Rector's family about who should pay for repairs to the house. Some parishes did not have a house and the Rector had to rent one which was sometimes unsuitable.

The system which had evolved to pay clergy was complicated, both to understand and to administer. Rectors received their income from three sources, tithes, Easter dues and surplice fees. The idea of tithes came from the Old Testament where each person gave one tenth of their income to support the priest. In theory, this was a good idea but by the early eighteenth century was proving difficult to manage. Farmers and landowners were expected to pay their tithes in kind so that in 1710[2] *'a tithe of corn is paid in kind with the fourth sheaf of all grain being given', one in ten fleeces of wool, one lamb in every ten, 1 milch cow in every ten, 2 eggs for each cockerel and one for each hen.'* This meant that each Rector had to have land and barns and probably help to manage the stock, and must have had a great deal of work collecting the tithes. Quite a number of land owners began to pay their tithes in money thus avoiding disputes over what to do if there were nine lambs not ten, for example. Those who were not landowners and farmers, paid a contribution every Easter. This was set down by the vestry and varied from parish to parish. In 1683[3] the 'Easter dues' in Cerrigydrudion were 5d for a married couple, 3d for widows and widowers and 2d for single people. Surplice fees were so named because, as well as wearing a black gown and white preaching tabs, the Rector wore a white surpice.

These services were weddings, funerals and churchings. In 1749[4] the fees in Betws Gwerfyl Goch were 5s for a wedding, 7d for a churching and the Report states *'it was customary to offer the Rector something at a funeral.'* This money was sometimes placed on the coffin at the end of the service. There was also a fee for reading the Banns before a wedding.

It is obvious that it was difficult from year to year to work out the total income as it depended on the vagaries of farming, the numbers of people who died, how many babies were born, who got married and the size of the population generally. In 1749 Evan Wynne, the Rector of Cerrigydrudion's stipend was £130. By 1807, the stipend was £450. In Llanfihangel Glyn Myfyr the stipend was £70 in 1749 and £120 by 1807.

Before becoming a Rector everyone would start their ministry as a Curate. Curates were those who had just been ordained, having usually attended a grammar school, such as Ruthin, Llanrwst or Wrexham and then gone on to a University College in either Oxford or Cambridge where they studied the Classics, Greek and Latin and a small amount of Theology. Normally, they were awarded their degree after three years and, assuming they were at least twenty two years old, were ordained by a Bishop. Unlike the situation now, men could be ordained without having a parish to go to. Curates were employed and paid by Rectors.

William Hughes was employed by David Wynne in Llanfihangel Glyn Myfyr from 1720 – 1729, probably because David Wynne was not well enough to carry out his parish duties.

Evan Wynne employed a series of curates to do most of the work in Cerrigydrudion because he was also Rector of Hope, near Wrexham. William Rowland was a fellow at Jesus College, Oxford, as well as being Rector in Cerrigydrudion from 1800 – 1820, and a variety of curates served here while he was in Oxford.

It was an uncertain existance as one's employment was dependant on the Rector not moving to another parish or dying!

We know little about the twenty five curates were in Cerrigydrudion between 1662 – 1812. Grifith Ellis who was curate from 1746 – 1754 married Barbara, a local girl, and their two children, Ellen and Richard, were baptised in church. *They lived in the church house in the Llan'.*5 The chapter called 'Meet the People' gives us an insight into another curate, Peter Powell.

It has been generally assumed that clergy in the eighteenth century were very poor and some, almost illiterate. To a certain extent this may have been true in south Wales, but in the two northern dioceses of Bangor and St Asaph , most clergy had an adequate stipend and curates managed on about £30 a year plus the surplice fees. Of the ten men who served as Rectors between 1662 – 1812 all went to university in Oxford, and, with the exception of James Price, all attended Jesus College. This is not surprising because it was known as 'the Welsh College' and men, especially from north Wales, wishing to take a degree were encouraged to go there. Of the twenty five curates, it has only been possible to find information out about nine, who all attended Jesus College. Because so many men from Wales were at the college a great deal of networking went on helping people to find curates and parishes. Rectors were appointed to parishes in a whole variety of ways. The Bishop of St Asaph appointed to some parishes including Cerrigydrudion, Llanfihangel Glyn Myfyr and Betws Gwerfyl Goch. Others, for historical reasons, were appointed by local landowners, Oxford and Cambridge Colleges, the Crown and assorted individuals who seemed to have no obvious links with the parish. This was still the system in Wales until disestablishment in 1920 and is still the system in England.

Having been appointed to a parish as a Rector, men could stay there for the rest of their lives unless they committed a serious crime, and even then it was quite difficult to have the person removed. In 1749, for example, the Rural Dean wrote of Evan Wynne, who was Rector from 1731 – 1757 'that he had been very wild in his youth, but was beginning to settle down. He suffered badly from gout'.[6]

The majority of the clergy came from similar backgrounds to their neighbours and fitted in well within the community. They were all Welsh-speaking and the services and church life generally was conducted entirely in Welsh. Every church had a Welsh Bible and Prayer Book, but many did not need an English Bible or Prayer Book.

The parish of Cerrigydrudion is very scattered and hilly and covers a wide area. This meant that clergy spent a lot of time travelling to outlying farms and houses on foot or horseback. They were expected to respond immediately to messages telling them that someone was ill or dying, as well as women who were having a difficult labour, meaning that their life, or the life of the baby was at risk. At home they would have had some servants, outside to help with the stock and land management and inside to help run the house. They would have had to spend time preparing a weekly sermon using the limited number of books available. Far more Christian books in Welsh became available by the middle of the eighteenth century, both commentaries on Bible passages and books such as 'The Pilgrim's Progress' by John Bunyon, were available and the Bishop of St Asaph had set up a Library of books for clergy to use.

It has been possible to draw up a diary for two different months which shows the basic tasks the Rector would have done.

FEBRUARY 1739

Sun 1st   Sacrament Sunday
       11.00   Mattins followed by Holy Communtion
       4.00   Evensong
               No Sermon today

Mon 2nd   Candlemas
       12.00   Service

Wed 4th 12.00   Funeral of John Meredith, Almshouses

Sun 8th   Quinquagesima
       11.00   Mattins and Sermon
       4.00   Evensong
               Published Banns of Marriage for Edward
               Wiliam and Lowry Roberts. Mary, wife of
               Thomas William, Tai'n Rhos was Churched

Wed 11th   Ash Wednesday
       12.00   Service
               Baptism of Elizabeth, daughter of Robert
               Morris and Anne, Glan Gors

Sun 15th   Lent 1
       11.00   Mattins and Sermon
               Began instructig the children in the Catechism
               Read Banns
       4.00   Evensong
Wed 18th   Baptism of Ellin, daughter of Cadwaladr Howel
               and ElizabethWilliam Cadwaladr, Hafod
               Dinbych

Sun 22nd	Lent 2
11.00	Mattins and Sermon
	Continued insruction in the Catechism
	Read Banns for the third time. No objections
	3 Churchings: Jane, wife of Robert Edward,
	Cwmpennaner, Dorothy, wife of Hugh
	Myddleton, Catherine, wife of William
	Cadwaladr.
4.00	Evensong
Tues 24th	St Matthias
12.00.	Service.
	Funeral of John, son of John Davies and Jane,
	Llaethwryd
	Baptism of Margaret, daughter of David
	Edward and Gwen, Hendre Bach
Wed 25th	Churching: Catherine, wife of Lewis David
Fri 27th	Wedding: Edward William and Lowry Robert
Sun 29th	Lent 3
11.00	Mattins Continued instruction
	Requested all those intending to make their
	communion the following Sunday to give me
	their names
4.00	Evensong

Evan Wynne was Rector during this period and must have taken some of these services while his curate took others.

The following shows a month after Easter when David Lloyd was Rector.

APRIL 1761

Wed 1st Two churchings: Lowry, wife of John Roberts, Hafod
y Maidd and Margaret, wife of Thomas Morgan, Cwm Main

Thurs 2nd   Meeting, held in the Alehouse, to distribute the
Thomas Parry Charity money..

Sun 5th   Easter 2, Sacrament Sunday
    11.00   Mattins followed by Holy Communion
    No Sermon
    Banns for John Davies, labourer, and Gwen
    William from Llanfihangel Glyn Myfyr
    Third time. No objections
    4.00   Evensong

Thurs 9th   Funeral of an infant, Edward Robert

Sat 11th   Wedding of John Daniel and Gwen William

Sun 12th   Easter 3
    11.00   Mattins and Sermon
    Funeral of Catherine Griffiths
    4.00   Evensong

Thurs 16th   Baptism of Lowry, daughter of Evan Ellis and
Lowry
Sun 19th   Easter 4
    11.00   Mattins and Sermon
    Banns of Robert Roberts, a labourer from
    Llanfor, and Mary Jones
    Churching of Jane, wife of Humphrey Cadwaladr
    4.00   Evensong

Mon 20th   Baptism of Ellis, son of John Wynne and Anne Ty'n y Myddun

Sat 25th   St Mark
     12.00 Service

Sun 26th   11.00   Mattins and Sermon
           Banns
           Funeral of Catherine Jones an infant
     4.00   Evensong

In 1784 James Price was appointed as the new Rector. He came from a wealthy,south Walian family and was one of the heirs to the Pwllycrochan Estate in Colwyn Bay.

His arrival marked a slow change in church life because he was very different from his predecessors and does not seem to have 'fitted in' as well. By the late 1780's he had organised the building of the new Rectory in the latest Georgian style.[7] It was a house suitable for a wealthy gentleman which stood out from all the other properties in the area and seems to have set him apart from his parishoners. In 1795 Edward Jones tried to raise a mob against the Rector. There are more details in the chapter on 'Meet the People'. Although services and church life were still conducted in Welsh, some people began to turn to the non-conformists because they were perceived to be more 'local and for the people'.

In 1800 William Rowland was appointed Rector. He was unable to live in the parish except for a brief spell during the summer because he was a fellow of Jesus College, Oxford. This meant that he was lecturing there most of the year and so appointed curates to fulfill his duties. We begin to see more use of English, for example, the children were taught the Catechism (a series of questions and answers about the Christian faith) in English. This seems to have been partly so that the Bishop who was not Welsh speaking, could understand. Unfortunately, the children would not have understood.

The Church was still playing an important role in peoples lives in 1812 but there are hints that it's influence was on the wane.

THE CLERGY
Rectors of Cerrigydrudion 1662 - 1812

Name	Dates	Degree/s
Robert Wynne	1660 – 1697	MA
Maurice Jones	1697 – 1725	BA, MA, BD
John Wynne	1725 – 1731	BA, MA
Evan Wynne	1731 – 1757	BA, MA
Thomas Price	1757 – 1760	MA
David Lloyd	1760 – 1763	BA
Humphrey Humphries	1763 – 1778	BA, MA
Ambrose Thelwell Lewis	1778 – 1784	BA, MA
James Price	1784 – 1800	BA
William Rowland	1800 - 1820	MA. Fellow

All the Rectors attended Jesus College, Oxford with the exception of James Price who went to Oriel College, Oxford. A BA was awarded after three years study, an MA was automatically given after another year, assuming the person to be working in some area vaguely defined as 'education'. A 'fellow' was someone on the staff at one of the colleges.

END NOTES

[1] NLW Rural Dean's Report for Penllyn and Edeyrnion. 1729
[2] NLW Terrier for Cerrigydrudion. 1710
[3] NLW Terrier for Cerrigydrudion. 1683
[4] NLW The state of the Church Report. 1749
[5] NLW Rural Dean's Report for Rhos Deanery. 1749
[6] NLW Rural Dean's Report for Rhos Deanery. 1749
[7] Drawing done by Mrs. Biddy Greenwood. 2000

Chapter 9

CERRIGYDRUDION CHURCH

St. Mary Magdalen Church in 1872.

This is a photograph of the church in 2011.[1]

According to a well substantiated tradition the disciples of St Patrick travelled from Ireland to Wales preaching the good news of Jesus Christ and establishing churches across Anglesey and mainland north Wales. They seem to have followed an ancient route similar to the present A5 and arrived in Cerrigydrudion in 440 AD. A small, probably wooden, church was built and dedicated to St Mary Magdalen. The services and organisation of the church were similar to those of the ancient Celtic Church in Ireland. As time went by a more permanent stone church was built with a circular churchyard, a sign of early Celtic foundation. Over the next thousand years the church would have been altered and developed and in 1503 *'it was repaired and augmented in ye time of Henry VII. Johannes ap Robert was then the Rector'*.[2] The window at the east end was that of 'Ieuan ap Lhewelch of Kinmeirch surnamed Gwas Patrick'. Some small fragments of glass from this window are preserved in a frame in the church.

Photo of the pieces of stained glass.[3]

By 1662 the stone building had a thatched roof and some small leaded windows which are still in the church. The floor was earthen and some backless wooden benches were placed in the nave. In 1576 a new bell had been cast with the words *'In the name of God, Amen, 1576'* written on it, and a second bell was cast by Mr Clybery of Holt, in 1640, costing £12-5s-6d.

Photo of the bell.[4]

Around 1640 a porch was added to the church, which must have helped keep some of the wind and cold out. The church had a wooden altar, a font and, in 1684, a new reading desk. The Price family of Geeler built a side chapel sometime around 1670 and Mr Thomas Price was buried there. His stone memorial can still be seen in the chapel as well as a very ornate memorial to Mrs Margaret Price.

The residents of the Almshouses used to sit in this side chapel. During the 1690s some repairs were carried out on the church and two men left money in their wills towards this work. John Roberts[6] of Ty'n Gilfach left 6s-8d and Robert David,[7] of Ty'n y Waen's will stated *'I give and bequeath for the repair of the church of Cerrigydrudion 30s provided I am promised to be buried within the said church'*.

The early part of the eighteenth century saw further improvements with rails placed around the altar in 1707 and a better pulpit added by 1713. The earthen floor, in common with

The Margaret Price stone memorial, Cerrigydrudion.[5]

most houses, was flagged with stone and the thatch repaired on a regular basis. Backless benches seem to have been the only seating provided and there is no evidence that any box pews were placed in the church. These pews were usually put in by wealthy, gentry families and by the 1730s there were no gentry families in the area.

In common with all churches after the Reformation the new Communion Service introduced in 1558 stated that people were to receive communion 'in both kinds'. For centuries the congregation had only received the bread with the priest alone taking the wine. Churches did not have a chalice large enough for this and so there was a need to buy a larger chalice. Some churches seem to have had one made fairly quickly others took time to find something more permanent.

The Chalice of Llanfihangel church made in Chester in 1575.[8]

Cerrigydrudion had a chalice made in 1615 inscribed with the words *'the cuppe of Cerrigydrudion'* and in 1725 the Rector, Revd Maurice Jones presented the parish with a new, flagon, which is still in use today.

From the mid 1750s onward the population began to grow and, even holding two services each Sunday, it was clear that the building was not large enough. On 5 April 1770 the Rector Humphrey Humphreys and the two churchwardens applied to the Diocese for permission to place a gallery at the back of the church which was to include a seat for the Rector's family. The new gallery seemed to solve the problem for the next twenty years but in 1792 people began to discuss whether the church

The flagon in Cerrigydrudion church.[9]

123

should be demolished and a larger one built. The Rural Dean[10] gave the following advice

'There is some idea of a new church because the present one is said to be too small to contain the parishioners. It is very difficult to make a more substantial masonry work. It will be very hard to demolish it, suppose the roof is raised, new regular windows made and a large gallery erected. I consider this would answer every purpose'.

Fortunately, this advice seems to have been taken and by 1800 a new slate roof had replaced the thatch and, as far as we know, the new gallery erected.

The 150 years between 1662 –1812 saw many changes to the church building. Some reflected the developments in domestic housing, such as the stone flagging of the floor and the slating of the roof, others were for practical reasons like the building of the gallery and a few were linked with the new thinking about worship in church, which led to the altar being placed against the east wall, rather than in the chancel, and railings being placed around it.

Until the 1880s the building had remained much the same but then the Victorians began major changes which are still evident today. In the early 1980s further work was done and in 2000 the church was re-roofed and the bells re-hung.

END NOTES

[1] Drawing from *'Architechural Antiquities and Village Churches in Denbighshire.'* Lloyd-Williams and Underwood.1872. Facsimilie copy made about 2000. p.25.
[2] A note in the Register for Cerrigydrudion.
[3] Photo taken by Myrddin ap Dafydd.
[4] Photo used with kind permission of Mr. E.Rowlands, Cerrigydrudion.
[5] Photo taken by Myrddin ap Dafydd.

[6]   NLW. SA/1695/94.
[7]   NLW. SA/1699/4.
[8]   Drawing by Mrs. B.Greenwood, Glasfryn. 2000.
[9]   Drawing by Mrs. B.Greenwood, Glasfryn. 2000.
[10] NLW. Rural Dean's Report. Rhos Deanery. 1795.

Chapter 10

THE RISE OF NON-CONFORMITY

One of the problems relating to the background to non-conformity and other areas of Welsh history, is that the majority of research has been done on south and mid Wales, and then an assumption made that what was found would be the same in north Wales. As far as the rise of non-conformity is concerned this has certainly been the case. The Church in the two Dioceses in south Wales, Llandaff and St.David's, were in a parlous state by the early eighteenth century. As was explained in the chapter about the Church,[1] clergy were paid through a complicated system of tithes and in south Wales most of these had been taken over by lay people leaving clergy to live on £10 or less each year. This meant that they had to look after three or four parishes which covered a large area and the task became impossible. Sunday Services took place when the Rector arrived, baptisms and funerals were difficult to orgainse and people became disallusioned with what was happening. Far more people used English or were familiar with the language than was true in north Wales and so, the visiting preachers coming from England who were the early Methodists, found many people able to understand their message and ready to accept it.

In north Wales the Church was still almost entirely Welsh speaking, except along the English/Welsh border. Records show that all services were conducted in Welsh and many Churches did not have an English language Bible or Prayer Book, *'because they had no need of them.'*[2] This was certainly true of Cerrigydrudion and the neighbouring parishes.

In 1681[3] the Bishop of St.Asaph sent a request to all clergy in the diocese to send him a list of all residents in the parish and to record of all dissenters and recrusants' (ie. Roman Catholics). David Wynne the Rector sent a letter to the Bishop stating that Mary Lloyd and Hugh ap Edward were non-conformists, but he had some hopes of bringing Mary Lloyd over to the Church for *'I find her more moderate than some of her brethren'. Hugh ap Edward was 'seldom in the parish' but 'resolute in his way'. Robert ap Rhyddech 'is the Quaker, a single man living with his sister an honest widow'.*

There were Quakers in the Bala and Cynwyd area and many of these chose to emigrate to America around the time of the Pilgrim Fathers, but there is hardly any evidence of any in the Cerrigydrudion area. The *Notitiae* for Betws Gwerfyl Goch stated, *'we have no Popish recrusants. Wee have one William John ap William, a Quaker, ye only dissenter in the parish, under excommuniation, has a daughter near three years old unbaptised'.*

One or two other people over the next thirty years or so were *'thought to be Quakers because of their apparall'*, Quakers tended to wear very plain, often black, clothes.

One test of whether a person was a member of the Church was if they attended Communion at Easter. Clergy and Churchwardens were often asked to provide a 'Sacrament Certificate' to state that someone had attended Comunion at Easter and suspicion might be raised if the person had no valid reason, such as sickness, for failing to attend Church at Easter. They were seen as not conforming to the Church.

As the non-conformist movement grew, meeting places were needed. They were not, until 1811 in Wales, seen as setting up a separate Church and so people wishing to set up an official or licensed meeting place filled in and signed a form to apply for permission from the Diocese. In the Diocese of St.Asaph there were almost no licences applied for before 1760 and very few before the late 1780s, although some people were meeting in unlicensed places.

By the end of the 1780s the Church in the area was beginning to be more 'English' in what was happening. Diocesan Bishops appointed to both St.Asaph and Bangor were not Welsh-speaking, and had little idea of the needs of rural, Welsh-speaking communities. James Price who was appointed Rector in 1784 came from a wealthy, south Walian family who owned the Pwllycrochan Estate in Colwyn Bay. Although he was Welsh speaking, his life-style was that of a wealthy gentleman, who had enough money to build a brand new Georgian Rectory which was a clear statement of grandure and distanced him from his parishoners.

In 1783 Thomas Charles move to Bala bringing with him the clear message of Methodism which he could communicate to people in Welsh. He introduced into this area the corner-stones of Methodism, the small groups which became known as Ysgol Sabboth and the Cyfarfod Gweddi (prayer meetings). These groups encouraged people to read the Bible and to pray together. At first they met in barns and houses with a room large enough to hold them and did not apply for a licence for an official meeting place, so that in 1795 the Churchwardens from Cerrigydrudion reported to the Bishop[4] *'There are Methodists in the parish but not very numerous and those of low rank. They have not increased in later years. They assemble at different places in the parish which are not licensed. Their teachers are not known to me. The same person very rarely attending above twice. They are, in general, of a quiet and orderly life'.*

Later that same year on 10 July 1795 the first application was made for a licensed meeting house in Cerrigydrudion at Pen y Bryn. The actual building used was just below Pen y Bryn[5] at Ty'n Rhyd. Six people signed the application which was granted. Two brothers, John and Thomas Parry, came from Llangwm and were active in setting up the Ysgol Sabboth, with four local men, three being farm workers, Edward Jones, Thomas Davies and John Edward and the sixth David Edward of Hendre Bach. He was one of the local leaders of the new 'Methodism', well-known for preaching in the local meeting houses and when a chapel was finally established in Pen y Bryn in 1811, he was one of the early members. When he was sixty six, in 1818, he was made the first deacon.[6]

Between 1795 – 1813 there were seven applications in all for meeting houses. In each case at lease six people signed, including some women. They described themselves as Protestant Dissenters, but His Majesty's loyal subjects. On 2 August 1799 an application was made for a meeting place in Cwmpennaner and the others followed on. 6 February 1800 Ty'n Pant in Cefn Brith, 1801 Ty Isaf (Lower Shop) in the Llan, 3 January 1796 in Rhyd y Gaeddren, 3 April 1866 in Pentrellyncymer where William Thomas is described as 'the minister' and then the meeting place in Rhyd y Gaeddren was moved and relicensed in Ty'n Gilfach on 7 May 1813. The house was 'now in the occupation of Hugh Evans, to be used as a place of worship. Hugh Evans was described as 'the minister' and a Thomas Ellis signed stating that he was a 'Dissenting minister of an Independant persuasion'.

The Churchwardens had continued to keep the Bishop informed, writing in 1799[7] that there was a sect called the Methodists. They are not very many and they come from the lowest order. They meet in a licensed place with itinerant preachers and are quiet and sober.' By 1806[8] they stated that 'there are twenty four persons belonging to a Society calling themselves the Calvanistic Methodists'.

Although the Churchwardens described the members as being of a lower rank this was not entirely accurate as quite a few of those who signed applications had themselves served as Churchwardens, including David Edwards, of Hendre Bach, and Overseers of the Poor.

Until 1811, the Methodists in Wales and in England had continued to see themselves as members of the Church, and Methodism a group within the Church, but relationships were very strained by then and in 1811 Thomas Charles,[9] in Bala and others, ordained twenty one men as ministers in the Methodist church and one of these was appointed to Pen y Bryn Chapel. The chapel was seen as a preaching house primarily but from 1812[10] a few people began to bring their children to be baptised, these included Jenkin Edward, a mason, and his wife Catherine Thomas who lived in the cottages near Pen y Bryn, and had eight children. with the last one being baptised there in 1815. Jeremiah Jones, a farmer from Tyn Braich, and his wife, Ann had their sickly daughter, Margaret. baptised on the day she was born 29 December 1811. She died a few days later and was buried in church. In December 1812 another daughter was baptised in Pen y Bryn. The most well-known early member was William Jones who signed the original faculty and came from Pen y Bryn. His parents were John Roberts and Catherine, from Ty'n Graig.

William Jones was a well-known builder who went to school in Chester and was one of the group of Welsh builders, known as the 'Liverpool Group' because of the large number of properties they built in Liverpool. William Jones was one of the instigators in the establishment of a permanent chapel building and he also purchased land to build a school and house which was to be

A plaque in Cerrigydrudion church placed by
William Jones, in memory of his parents.[11]

financed from the income gained from Pen y Bryn farm. The
school eventually became the local infant school. It seems that
from the beginning the tradition of offering the preachers
hospital was established and Kitty Davies of Ty'n Rhyd was
mentioned, *'byddai y pregethwyr yn lletya yn nhy gwraig dra
ffyddlon, sef Kitty Davies'.*[12]

We need to remember that until 1834 when public
registration was brought in, the only record of people's birth,
marriage and death, was the one kept by the church. When Pen
y Bryn Chapel was established a Baptism Book was kept but
discontinued in 1835 after public registration, as people had to
register the birth of their children. Marriages were legal
transactions which could only take place in church where the
Rector was the registrar and funerals were also seen as a legal
matter, and so it was not until the 1880s that funerals were

allowed to take place in chapels. Churches were built with a central aisle to facilitate couples walking 'up the aisle' together and coffins being carried to the Chancel during the service, whereas early chapels were built as preaching houses with plenty of pews for the congregation and no need to provide for the space needed to conduct a wedding or a funeral.

By 1812 then, Cerrigydrudion had one newly established Calvanistic Methodist Chapel at Pen y Bryn, and a number of licensed meeting places which soon became chapels in Cwmpennaner, Cefn Brith and Pentrellyncymer.

END NOTES

[1] NLW. Rural Dean's, and other Reports for the Diocese of St. David's and Llandaff.

[2] NLW. Rural Dean's Reports for the Deaneries of Rhos, and Penllyn and Edeyrnion. 1710-1749.

[3] DRO. *The Notitiae*. These are also available on CD.ROM.

[4] NLW. Churchwardens' Reports for the Deanery of Rhos. 1795.

[5] NLW. Faculty Application Book. Diocese of St. Asaph. 1770-1828.

[6] W.Williams. 'Methodisiaeth Dwyrain Merionydd,' Davies and Evans, Bala. 1902.

[7] NLW. Churchwardens' Report for Cerrigydrudion. 1799.

[8] NLW. Churchwardens'Report for Cerrigydrudion. 1806.

[9] W. Williams. *Methodistiarth Dwyrain Merionydd*. Davies and Evans. Bala. 1902.

[10] DRO. Bptism Book for Ty'n Rhyd Chapel.

[11] Photo taken by Myrddin ap Dafydd.

[12] W. Williams. *Methodistiaeth Dwyrain Merionydd*. Davies and Evans. Bala. 1902.

Chapter 11

MEET THE PEOPLE

Two spinsters; Martha Williams and Margaret Jones
An Apprentice; Lewis Hughes
Blacksmith's family; Edward Thomas ap Hugh
Parish Clerks; Lewis Annwyl, Lewis Lloyd
The family at Ty Coch; Edward Cadwlaladr and Magdalen David
A troublemaker; Edward Jones
A curate; Peter Powell

Thousands of names appear in the parish registers and other documents about this period and many of them are just names. However, a few people stand out because there is more information about them and this enables us to have a glimpse into the lives of a few people in more depth.

The Two Spinsters:- Martha Williams and Margaret Jones

We know very little about the lives of either of these women except that they did not marry and lived independently. Both left wills and in Martha Williams' case there was also an inventory.

Martha Williams

Martha Williams was buried on the 6 March 1752 and the register adds that she was an old maiden lady believed from Ty Tan y Graig. She actually lived in Cae Corwch but probably moved to Ty Tan y Graig to be with a member of her family. In her will she leaves her two nephews, Williams and Thomas Jones and two nieces Magdalen and Margaret Jones, £1 each. These would have

Inventory Martha Williams

All her bed linen	10-00
One chest	2-06
One old table	1-00
Little pan	-06
One bedstead and small	
things in her room	5-00
Two cows	4-10-00
Money at interest	7-10-00
	12-19-00

been her sister's children and to her brother Hugh's children, William and Robert also £1 each and the rest of her estate to her brother Hugh, who was executor.

Two months later on 7th May 1752 Llewelyn Hughes and Edward Jones met to make an inventory of her possessions. She seems to have lived in a one roomed cottage, with a lean to attached where her two cows, valued at £4, were kept. In the house were 'bed cloaths' worth 10-0d, a chest, probably for keeping oats, valued at 2s-6d, one 'old table' worth 1s-0d, a 'little pan' worth 6d and 'one bedstead and other things in the room' valued at 5s-0d. This gives us a picture of her household and a glimpse into her life. She, like many single women, earned money by lending it out at interest and the inventory records that the money lent out when she died was £7 -10 s- 0d.

Margaret Jones

Margaret Jones lived at Golden Gro. Her will[2] was made on 26 February 1762 but she went on to live another seven years, being buried on 14 June 1769. She was clearly a much wealthier woman than Martha Williams with a large family living locally and in neighbouring communities including Bala. She left money, as follows;

Brother William	1 s– 0d. Prayer Book
Sister Mary	12 s– 0d
Nephew William Jones from Dolgynlas	5 s– 0d
Niece Catherine, Rhyd y Kilgwyn	£5
Niece Gwen	£1
Niece Susan, wife of Peter Evans, Bala	£1
Nephew Thomas	£1
Great nephews and niece Hugh, William, Gwen	£1 between them when they are 21
Godson John Owen	5s – 0d
Niece Margaret Lloyd	£2 when she is 21 or married
Nephew Richard	£2
Nephew Thomas	£5
Niece Anne	£2
Elizabeth	£2
Mary Williams	£4 and my wainscot chest

To her sister, Mary, she left the use of her iron pot and frying pan for life and then to Anne William, a daughter of Elizabeth Lloyd. She also left Anne her wearing apparal, £3 and a chest of drawers, a feather bed, bolster, bedstead, sheets, blanket and quilt.

To her niece, Elizabeth Lloyd, the use of the rest of her household goods for life, and then to be given to Anne Williams.

The rest of her estate was to be given to her nephew William Lloyd, who was also the executor.

The will gives a picture of someone who was part if a close family and wanted to remember all her nieces and nephews as well as her great nephews and nieces. She left nearly £30 to her family as well as some of her treasured possessions. Her brother received her Prayer Book and others, a chest of drawers and a wainscot chest. This was a decorated chest. It highlights the value placed on clothes and on cooking utensils. Elizabeth Lloyd, who received a bed and bedding would have valued this as part of her 'bottom drawer' for when she got married.

There is no indication of how Margaret Jones acquired her money. Possibly, she, with others, farmed the land around Golden Gro.

The Apprentice :- Lewis Hughes

Lewis Hughes was baptised on 1 January 1747, the fifth child of Hugh Cadwaladr Jenkin, a hosier, and Elin Williams, who lived in Rhyd y Cae. When Lewis was eleven his father died. With the death of his father the family were left in difficult circumstances, and the Thomas Parry charity for 1760 states 'it is hereby promised that Lewis Hughes, a poor child of the parish, shall have £1 – 10s of this towards him doing an apprenticeship as a tailor.' So in 1760, aged thirteen, Lewis began his training with Cadwaladr Hughes. He may well have gone to live with Cadwaladr Hughes' family during the time.

In 1761 he received 15s and 10s over each of the next three years. His mother had managed to stay in the family home and by

1768, now aged twenty-one, Lewis was living there and making his living as a tailor. On 17 December 1768, Lewis' illegitimate child, Thomas, was baptised, the mother being named as Elinor Williams. Sadly Thomas died three weeks later. Lewis did not marry Elinor probably, at least in part, because he had only just completed his training. He got married on 9 March 1770 to Jane Thomas from Gyffylliog, and they went on to have three children, Thomas, William and Lewis. Three months after the birth of Lewis, Jane died. Within a relatively short time, he remarried another girl also called Jane Thomas from Llangwm. They had a further four children, Cadwaladr, Elizabeth, Ellin and John. Lewis seems to have managed to maintain his family from his work as a tailor. At some point they moved to Gors Llewelyn and he was still working, aged sixty three in 1812.

The Blacksmith's Family: - Edward Thomas ap Hugh

Edward Thomas ap Hugh was married on 20 June 1733 in Cerrigydrudion Church to Dulcibella Jones from Betws Gwerfyl Goch. He was the blacksmith in Cerrigydrudion, and his business was situated in the Llan just onto the Denbigh Road. Over the next twenty years, they had nine children.

The first William died at about a year old. It may have been that he was a handicapped baby, because another blacksmith, Roberts Evan, who died in early 1741 left Edward Thomas and Williams, his son, 40s to be divided between them.

John, the eldest son, was apprenticed to his father and joined the family business. On 27 September 1756, he married Jane Jones and they had seven children.

Thomas, the second son was fifteen when his father died in June 1753. He was already serving his apprenticeship at this time and continued working with John, his brother, In 1759 he

Edward Thomas ap Hugh and Dulcibella Jones

John 18.12.33
Ellin 12.03.35
Thomas 23.06.38
William 27.09.40
Jane 12.08.42
William 06.03.44
Margaret 23.03.46
Douse 30.06.49
Robert 20.05.53

received £1 towards his training from the Thomas Parry Charity and a further 10s in 1760. On 4 February 1764 he married Mary Davies of Pentrellyncymer and, having completed his apprenticeship, set up a business in Pentrellyncymer. The population in this area was beginning to grow and by the middle of the eighteenth century the horse had almost completely replaced the ox as a working animal on the farm. A number of inventories mention horses, such as John Davies,[3] of Llaethwryd, who died in 1729, he owned *'2 horses, other horses, 1 grey mare, 2 fillies, 2 horses and one other horse.'* The inventory of John Pugh,[4] of Blaen Cwm, listed *'2 mares, 2 fillies, 2 saddles and 2 panniers and 8 other panniers.'* These horses were used for riding and the panniers, which were large baskets, would have been fitted either side of the saddle, and filled with goods to be sold in local markets. Besides the work shoeing horses, blacksmiths made many metal goods such as gate hinges, scythe blades, ploughshares, hooks to hang cooking pots, axes and pitchforks. They would also have been called on to mend items.

The inventory of Evan David,[5] a yeoman from Elor Garreg, who died in 1755, included *"2 turf spades(for digging peat for the fire), 1 garden spade. 1 iron link, a pair of iron fetters, 2 scythes and some chains,'* all of which were probably made by the local blacksmith.

In 1756 a court case is recorded concerning the theft of a gelding valued at 40s (£2).[6] The gelding had been stolen at a horse fair in Llanrwst by Ffoulk William. The horse was found in Llanelian and Ffoulk William was apprehended in Llanrwst. As the local blacksmith John Edward was called to identify the horse, but in spite if there being three witnesses, Owen Jones, Hugh Evans of Tau Ucha, Cwm and Lawrence Jones of Glan Gors. Ffoulk Williams was found to be not guilty.

John Edward and Thomas Edward, the two elder sons were able to sign their names when they got married in 1756 and 1764 indicating some level of literacy. It was very unlikely that either boy went to Grammar School and so must have learnt to write at home or within the community.

Dulcibella was widowed in June 1753 a month after Robert, their youngest son was born, leaving her with a number of dependant children, although the two eldest sons, John and Thomas, were working as blacksmiths by then. It is not clear how the family managed financially but she did not die until May 1794, forty years after her husband. Her name is very unusual and was probably a variation of the more common name Douse, her youngest daughter was called Douse. She may well have been a godmother to the other person called Dulcibella. She was the daughter of Peter Roberts and Alice who started married life in the Llan near to the blacksmith's house and was baptsed on 15 August 1736. The family later moved to Pant Dedwydd.

The other children of Edward Thomas and Dulcibella all married people from Cerrigydrudion and remained living within the parish.

The Parish Clerks: Lewis Anwyl, Lewis Lloyd, Thomas Jones

The Parish Clerk was appointed by the Vestry Meeting on Easter Monday, but whereas other positions were appointed annually the Parish Clerk served for many years. They took an active part in church services singing part of the service and maybe reading the Bible passages. They also had to keep a detailed record of all baptisms, weddings and funerals sending off a copy each year to the Bishop, for which they were paid a small sum. Reports made by the Rural Deans seem to indicate that some of these clerks were elderly and incompetent, but this was certainly not the case in Cerrigydrudion.

Lewis Anwyl, a gentleman from Tai yn y Foel served for many years and a plaque on the wall to the left of the altar in the church reads, 'Underneath lieth the remains of Lewis Anwyl of Tai yn y Foel, Gent'.

In 1741 he was listed on the register of electors and freeholders and was buried on 4 March 1765, aged ninety one.

On 29 August 1757 Lewis Lloyd, Aged 33 of Ty Tan y Foel was

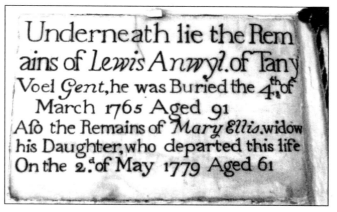

Photo of the plaque.[7]

licensed by the Diocese of St Asaph as the new Parish Clerk to succeed Lewis Anwyl. In 1767 he married Elinor Davies and they went on to have five children. Lewis Lloyd was probably the son of Cadwaladr Lloyd and Jane Parry of Llyn y Cymmer, who was baptised on 7 August 1724 and continued as Parish Clerk until his death, aged 70, in September 1794. The parish register notes that he was Parish Clerk for 'upwards of forty years'. He was followed as Parish Clerk by Thomas Jones who combined the role with that of running an alehouse now known as the White Lion.

All three men wrote and witnessed a number of wills as well as witnessing many of the weddings. They were well educated and able to communicate in both written and spoken Welsh and English as the situation demanded.

Picture of the Licence issued for Lewis Lloyd by the
Diocese of St. Asaph.[8]

The Family at Tŷ Coch

Tŷ Coch was a house situated behind the alehouse (later known as The Queens). On 21st May 1708 Edward Cadwaladr and Magdalen David were married in Cerrigydrudion church and moved into Tŷ Coch. During their long marriage of fifty years they had eleven children. There is no record of their eldest son David's baptism but the others are all listed as follows;

Name	Date Baptised	Date Buried	Age at Burial
Elizabeth	11.10.1711	23.01.1713	15 months
Jane	25.11.1712	05.01.1713	2 weeks
Cadwaladr	01.11.1714	06.12.1721	7 years
Thomas	01.02.1716	26.11.1721	5 years
Elizabeth	25.03.1719		
William	No date	18.12.1721	Infant
Robert	11.07.1721	Died before 1763	
Jane	19.04.1723		
Cadwaladr	26.06.1724	18.12.1730	6 years
William	19.03.1726	09.02.1728	23 months

The list tells a sad story of a family who lost so many children. Elizabeth and Jane died in January 1713 and in 1721 with a six month old baby, Robert, in the house, three more children died between 26 November and 18 December. No reasons are given for the death of any of these children. It may be that they caught an infectious disease, but it must have placed the family under a great deal of strain. Edward Cadwaladr was a yeoman farmer and, as well as dealing with his family problems was serving as a churchwarden during 1721 and 1722. He was clearly someone active in the community and acted as the appraiser making the inventory of Edward Thomas of Bwlch y Beudy in 1732 and as both appraiser and executor for the estate of Jane David, his sister in law, widow of Willilam Prichard of Hendre Bach.

In 1736, his eldest son, David, was married to Gwen Thomas from Llanfihangel Glyn Myfyr and they went to live in Hendre Bach.

Towards the end of 1743 Edwards Cadwaladr, his wife Magdalen David, and his son Robert Edward[9] were summoned to appear at the next Quarter sessions in Ruthin to answer a charge of 'assault' and 'battery' against Thomas Prichard. It is possible that Thomas Prichard was a brother of William Prichard, the late brother-in-law of Magdalen. We know nothing else about Thomas Prichard except that he died in 1752 in Cappele. No indication is given of the outcome of this case but three men of standing from the village signed a bond promising that the three accused would keep the peace and they put aside a sum of money to guarantee this. The three men were Andrew Jones of Hafod y Maidd, Owen Robert of Creggiau Bleiddiau and Evan Jones from Hafod y Llan Isa.

No more is known of this family. Edward Cadwaladr died in 1763 leaving his two daughters, Elizabeth and Jane £10 each in his will, with £10 to be shared between his son David's children and naming his wife and eldest grandson Edward as executors. His wife Magdalen, died in 1768.

A Trouble Maker – Edward Jones

Edward Jones was a cousin of Jac Glan Gors. Although originally from Llechwedd Llyfn he seems to have moved to the Llan by 1793. After his court appearances in 1795 he seems to have been in custody until 1800 when he was back living in Llechwedd Llyfn.

He is first mentioned as one of the three men, who in 1789, were stirring up trouble in the parish. Along with Jac Glan Gors were Edward and William Lloyd of Bryn Heilyn It was suggested that the militia be called in to conscript the three young men. They objected, saying that they would demolish the newly built Rectory. When the militia arrived from Corwen they had a meal, and then began their search in farms and outbuildings, but failed totally to find any of the three men. Jac, we know made his way to London, but Edward and William seem to have disapeared.

The Reverend James Price, the Rector, was a very wealthy gentleman and by 1795 had been made Justice of the Peace. This meant that he had to deal with the legal cases in the area.

In 1793 Edward Jones moved from Llechwedd Llyfn to the Llan, where he became a shop keeper. News of riots and of the growing Republican movement in France reached the community, and on Saturday 11 April 1795 he attempted to get local innkeeper, Hugh Davies, to go with him to incite a riot against the Rector. Hugh Davies refused and went to the Rector to tell him what had happened, stating[10]

"He is afraid that Edward Jones will do him some bodily harm. He is not praying out of malice, vexation or ill-will but merely the fear of his life or some bodily harm. He made a threat on the morning of Saturday 11th April and after talking a good deal, he said to Hugh David that their Parson (Revd. James Price) looked like a mob himself. What if we were to get some people together with him for he is so high-minded that he is above everybody and is got too great a man in our parish. Hugh Davies then asked him what his purpose was and what excuse he would have to get people together, to which Edward Jones replied, 'only say there are

*sheep in the pinfold and we shall have plenty of company'.
And the said Hugh Davies further said that he then asked the
said Edward Jones why he did not go to Thomas of Tŷ Du
and John the Smith, whereon the said Edward Jones left and
went to Rhyd y Groes and there the examinent followed him
and in the presence of Edward Jones and told John
Cadwaladr the Smith of Rhyd Groes of the intend of Edward
Jones of collecting a mob to mob the parson and the said
John Cadwaladr said it was not right and Edward Jones
went his way"*

A second statement was made by Evans Evans, a slater who
lived in the Llan, which said,[11]

*"Thomas William came to his house on Saturday 11 April at
about 2.00 in the evening and compelled him to leave the
plough and go and collect people from Llangwm. He had
asked why they were wanted and Thomas William had said
that they were to mob the parson, but that he was not to
inform the people he was to collect those who sent him. He
was to tell them to assembly at 5.00. These were the servants
from Tyn y Mynydd, Moelfre and Hendrearddwyfaen.
Thomas William wanted twelve men and procured them
from the upper end of the parishes Ysbyty Ifan, Tir Abbot
and Cerrigydrudion. Evan Evans told the mob to disperse
and that these were 'mischievious designs' proposed by
Thomas Williams.*

It appears that Thomas Williams was a labourer at Tŷ Du in 1795.

Besides this case, Edward Jones was also facing charges for
assault and on 14 July he made a hand written statement in
Welsh which read,[12]

*"Rhybydd, os oes gin neb ddim drwg iw ddweud am Edward
Jones o Llechwedd Llyfn nai glowod nai weled nai feddwl
dudodd i Mr Price foru ne dreunedd ne y bore ddiw mawrth
nesa ein iddo gochwen ir chwarter i rhoi yn aiewn oflaen y
dun i fod o un ddun drwg i gaol iddo fo golli fowod."*

(Notice: Warning. If anyone has anything bad to say about
Edward Jones, of Llechwedd Llyfn, whether heard or seen or
thought, say it to Mr. Price tomorrow, or the day after or next
Tuesday, so that he may start to the Quarters [Quarter
Sessions] so that he can place the complaints before the man
that he is a bad man to be sentenced to loose his life.)

This was signed by Revd..James Price as the hand writing of
Edward Jones.

When the case came up in court, both Edward Jones and
Williams Thomas were discharged because there was insufficient
evidence.

On 20 June, Edward Jones was again in trouble, this time for
*'beating, wounding and ill-treating Evan Williams so that his
life was despaired of.'* Evan Williams was a neighbour of Edward
Jones. He had been married to Mary Evans in 1755 and lived in
one of the three houses owned by the church in the Llan. He
worked as a stonemason. Edward Jones had a clear dislike of the
Rector, and this may well have extended to the church and those
living in church properties. He pleaded not guilty but the jury
found him guilty. By the 1 July he was again bound over 'to be of
good behaviour especially towards Jane, wife of Edward Wynne
of Ty'n Llidiart, a labourer. He seems to have ignored this and on
14 July Jane accused him of 'attempting to have carnal knowledge
of her'. She made a lengthy statement to Revd. James Price as
follows,[13]

"*Last spring twelve month Edward Jones came to the house, Castell at Llangwm, and asked her to come with him to the Votty and suffer him to have carnal knowledge of her body, but she refused to go and sometime afterwards, as she was returning to her home from Cerrigydrudion she accidentally met with the said Edward Jones on the hill of Melin Bwlch in the Parish of Llanfihangel and the said Edward Jones then seized her and threw her down on the bank against her inclination and used his endeavours to have carnal knowledge of her body and she verily believes that he would have attained his end had it not been for a man who appeared in an adjoining field in sight of the said Edward Jones and woman.*

And the said Edward Jones when he saw the man desisted his pursuits against her. Her strength was so exhausted with struggling with the said Edward Jones, that she was unable further to resist him and therefore he had so far attained his end as to have her coats up and his breeches down and had it not been that the said man appeared she believed that Edward Jones would have had carnal knowledge of her. She further saith to your worships that the said Edward Jones hath oft since attempted to have carnal knowledge of her body though to no effect and as late as Thursday 18th June he repeated his desires to her to go along in private and she is afraid that he will do her some bodily harm."

Her mark is at the bottom of the document. In spite of this detailed statement court reports indicate that Edward Jones was acquitted.

Edward Jones stands out as a persistent offender. It is difficult to know the background to these cases. It may be that living in the Llan adjacent to the alehouse contributed to his problems.

A Curate – Peter Powell

We know very little about the men who served as curates generally. Once someone had been ordained they would look for a Rector who would employ them. They were paid by the Rector and did some of the work in the parish. During the eighteenth century there were a good number of curates but Peter Powell is the only one we know much about. He was born in Ruthin in 1695, the son of William Powell. It is likely that he attended Ruthin School before going to Jesus College Oxford in March 1715. He was awarded his BA on 19 March 1719 and an MA in 1721. In 1720 he was ordained Deacon and was employed by Maurice Jones, the Rector in Cerrigydrudion. On 1st May 1724 he married a local woman, Margaret Thomas, in St Mary Magdalen church. He probably lived in a house next to The Queens which was owned by the church. During his time in Cerrigydrudion he wrote a series of sermons, some of which remain in a calf bound book kept in the National Library of Wales. There are nine sermons in the book, all written in Welsh with the dates that he preached each sermon carefully noted down. The book is about 7 inches wide by 9 inches long and each sermon is about nine pages long.

The first three sermons are based on a text from Diarhebion 1:10 *'fy mab, os pecharduriaid a'th ddenant, na chytuna.'* (Proverbs 1:10, 'my son, if sinners entice thee, consent thou not'). This sermon was preached on 9 December 1721 and 16 August 1724.

Picture of one page from this book.[14]

The next sermon, which was twenty pages long, was based on a text from Mathew 11:30, *'canys fy iau sydd esmwyth, a'm balch sydd ysgafn.'* (Mathew 11:30 'for my yoke is easy, and my burden is light'). This was preached on 12 August 1722 and 30 August 1724.

In 1726 Maurice Jones moved to another parish, which meant that Peter Powell also had to move. He became the Rector of Llanycil and was described by the Rural Dean in 1730 as follows, *"he is a very sober, industrious man of exemplary life and conduct, and one of the few, very few deserving clergymen in the Deanery of Penllyn and Edeyrnion'* [15]. In 1731 he was made a Canon of St Asaph Cathedral and in 1732 Rural Dean of Penllyn and Edeyrnion. He moved to be Rector of Llanrhaeadr ym Mochnant in 1736 and Llanymynech in 1749. His book of sermons notes the dates he preached these sermons in both Llanycil and Llanrhaeadr ym Mochnant.

END NOTES

[1] NLW. SA/1752/15.
[2] NLW. SA/1769/17/
[3] NLW. SA/1729/26.
[4] NLW. SA/1737/15.
[5] NLW. SA/1755/12.
[6] NLW. GSR/4/52/1.
[7] The plaque is on the wall to the left of the altar. Photo taken by Myrddin ap Dafydd.
[8] NLW. Bishop of St Asaph's Papers
[9] DRO. QSD/SR/139/31.
[10] DRO. QSD/SR/342/35.
[11] DRO. QSD/SR/342/33.
[12] DRO. QSD/SR/342/32.
[13] DRO. QSD/SR/
[14] NLW. In the collection of Bob Owen, Croesor
[15] NLW. Rural Dean's Report for Penllyn and Edeyrnion. 1730.

Chapter 12

END PIECE

If this book has helped to put together some of the pieces in the jigsaw for the reader, then it has done its job. There may still be pieces to be found, but some have been lost forever. If you want to read a little more then E.R.Millward's book on Jac Glan Gors is available, as is Idris Evan's Book about the drovers. Although long out of print there are copies of hugn Evan's book Cwm Eithin (The Gors Glen.) The end notes mention a number of other books and documents and these are available in the Denbighshire Record Office or The National Library of Wales.

Thank you again to all those who helped in any way to assemble this jigsaw.